One Week Loan

DATE DUE FOR R

Richard Titmuss:
Welfare and Society

Studies in Social Policy and Welfare
Edited by R. A. Pinker

I. Reforming the Welfare: The Politics of Change in the Personal
Social Services
Phoebe Hall

II. Universality, Selectivity, and Effectiveness in Social Policy
Bleddyn Davies

III. Richard Titmuss: Welfare and Society
David Reisman

IV. Rationing Social Services: A Study of Resource Allocation
in the Personal Social Services
Ken Judge

V. Violence and the Social Services in Northern Ireland
John Darby and Arthur Williamson

Richard Titmuss:
Welfare and Society

David Reisman

H·E·B

Heinemann : London

Published by Heinemann Educational Books Ltd

LONDON EDINBURGH MELBOURNE AUCKLAND
TORONTO HONG KONG SINGAPORE KUALA LUMPUR
NEW DELHI NAIROBI JOHANNESBURG LUSAKA
IBADAN KINGSTON

ISBN 0 435 82749 9
Paperback ISBN 0 435 82750 2
© David Reisman 1977
First published 1977

Published by Heinemann Educational Books Ltd
48 Charles Street, London WIX 8AH
Printed in Great Britain by
Richard Clay (The Chaucer Press) Ltd
Bungay, Suffolk.

Contents

Abbreviations of books by R. M. Titmuss

CW   *Commitment to Welfare* (London: George Allen and Unwin Ltd., 1968).

Cost   *The Cost of the National Health Service* (Cambridge: the University Press, 1956).

EWS   *Essays on 'The Welfare State'*, 2nd ed., (London: George Allen and Unwin Ltd., 1963).

GR   *The Gift Relationship* (Harmondsworth: Penguin Books, 1973).

HST   *The Health Services of Tanganyika* (London: Pitman Medical Publishing Co. Ltd., 1964).

IDSC   *Income Distribution and Social Change* (London: George Allen and Unwin Ltd., 1962).

IS   *The Irresponsible Society* (Fabian Tract 323, 1960, reprinted in *EWS*).

PSP   *Problems of Social Policy* (London: His Majesty's Stationery Office and Longmans, Green and Co., 1950).

SP   *Social Policy* (London: George Allen and Unwin Ltd., 1974).

SPPGM   *Social Policies and Population Growth in Mauritius* (London: Methuen and Co. Ltd., 1961).

Preface

After the obituaries, an uneasy silence usually follows the premature demise of a great scholar. It is a silence occasioned partly by deference and partly by uncertainty as to whether or not the time is yet ripe for critical review. In the case of Richard Titmuss the problem is compounded by the fact that during his lifetime his work was only very rarely subjected to reappraisal by other scholars within the discipline of social policy and administration. This deficiency may be explained, in large part, by the fact that few scholars have so dominated the development of an academic subject over so long a period of time as did Richard Titmuss. He was one of those rare thinkers who are able to shift the whole focus of debate in a field of study and thereby open up entirely new areas of intellectual enquiry. In his seminal essay, 'The Social Division of Welfare', Titmuss broke through the then conventional and narrow definitions of social policy and, by focusing upon aims rather than administrative procedures, he brought a new analytical dimension to his subject.

In my own reading of Titmuss I have come to admire most those works such as *Problems of Social Policy* and his studies of developing countries in which his enquiries ranged across a broad historical and societal canvas. Of his many essays, the two which most clearly demonstrate this quality are 'The Position of Women' and 'The Social Division of Welfare', both of which were published in *Essays on 'The Welfare State'*. In *Problems of Social Policy*, he explored the relationship between familial forms of social solidarity and the making of social policies in wartime Britain. In this great work, Titmuss demonstrated his remarkable capacity for organizing quantitative data and using it to illustrate aspects of the quality of social life. Similarly, in his analyses of social needs and policies in new nations such as Mauritius and Tanzania, he demonstrated with percipience and authority the dilemmas of choice and value in social policy.

When writing about the social problems of wartime Britain and the third world, Titmuss identified events and trends in social policy which allowed him to anticipate with a measure of real hope the eventual realization of his own political ideals. His last major work, *The Gift Relationship*, exemplifies another important element in the development of Titmuss' scholarship and one which became increasingly dominant towards the end of his life. *The Gift Relationship* is an essay in international welfare within which he set out what he believed to be the distinctive welfare ethic of the social market with its emphasis upon the 'universal stranger' and the integrative functions of social policy. I suspect, however, that in the last analysis Titmuss' true genius lay, not so much in making explicit the international dimensions of social welfare but in his searching exploration of the role of social policy in the recovery and maintenance of national consensus.

Much of the sense of moral purpose which inspired Titmuss' best work finds its parallel in the writings of R. H. Tawney. In many ways Titmuss inherited Tawney's ideals of a new socialist commonwealth and his policy choices can be seen as practical directives towards that end. Tawney's socialism was deeply imbued with Christianity and whilst Titmuss was ostensibly a secular thinker there are many parts of *The Gift Relationship* which have close ethical affinities with the traditions of Christian socialism.

The Gift Relationship is an assertion of the moral superiority of one form of welfare provision to another, based on Titmuss' premise that social policy 'extends opportunities for altruism in opposition to the possessive egoism of the market place'. The terms on which blood is donated and received are taken as one of the 'ultimate tests of where the "social" begins and the "economic" ends'. A free transfusion system is superior not simply because it is more efficient but because it fosters social integration and positively encourages altruism.

There is a close relationship between Titmuss' three models of social welfare, described in *Social Policy*, and the eight-point typology of donor types which he sets out in *The Gift Relationship*. The residual welfare and industrial achievement models are governed by moral criteria which are so alike that they can be treated for all but practical purposes as identical. Only the institutional redistributive model operates 'outside the market on the principle of need'. Titmuss' scrutiny of his eight donor types is extremely severe in its judgement of intentions. In effect all but one, the voluntary community donor, are shown to have their moral affinities with either the residual or the industrial achievement models of social welfare. The universe of the institutional redistributive model would find its natural citizens only among those who share the values of the voluntary community donor. In *The Gift Relationship* Titmuss sought to demonstrate the interrelationship of social structure, human nature and moral behaviour. He argued that in industrial societies there was a far greater scope for gift relationships than had previously been recognized and that citizens possess considerable potentialities for altruistic behaviour of that kind which can be either nurtured or destroyed under the influence of the dominant values of their society. Titmuss chose blood donorship as his test case because it goes beyond the limitations of family, community and class to encompass the universal stranger, and it is in our treatment of the universal stranger that altruism finds its true and fullest expression.

There are, however, at least three points at which Titmuss' approach is open to question. In the first place, he uses the terms 'altruism' and 'egoism' in such a way as to describe a polarity of sentiments and motives, which in the real world are more likely to be interactive and conditional. In their extreme forms altruism and egoism are marginal phenomena. The family may inspire a form of altruism which is very limited but which none the less motivates all of us at some time and may often lead us into conflict with redistributive social policies. A dichotomous model which allows familial altruism to be subsumed under the heading of 'egoism' is misleading. When he writes primarily as a social historian or as an analyst of specific social policy issues, Titmuss accords the family a very central position in his moral universe and shows much sensitivity towards the ambivalences of feeling and loyalty which the family generates as a social institution. When he writes primarily as a philosopher of social policy these issues of feeling and loyalty tend to become lost in a dichotomous division of the world into egoists inspired by the values of the economic market and altruists inspired by those of the social market.

The example of blood donorship fails to bring out the full complexity of the phenomenon of altruism. The fact that blood is a gift which costs us nothing is far more important than the fact that in some countries the sale of blood can be profitable. A more searching test of the scope and limits of altruism would be the donation of bodily organs the loss of which will place the donor's life or health in jeopardy. Most adults would unhesitatingly donate a kidney to a needful spouse or child. In some societies this sense of kinship might include more distant kin. In any society, however, a potential donor would have to consider very carefully the extent to which he is morally justified in placing at risk the welfare and security of his own family in order to save the life of a stranger. It is therefore by no means self-evident that altruistic acts on behalf of strangers are morally superior to altruistic acts on behalf of one's immediate kin. That there is a dimension of depth as well as breadth in the quality of altruism only serves to heighten the dilemma. Much depends on the nature of the goods or services in question.

Secondly, Titmuss' concepts of altruism and egoism so elevate the institutions of the social market and debase those of the economic market as to give the impression that the main effect of industrialism and entrepreneurial activity has been the infliction upon humanity of 'diseconomies and diswelfares'. Much of Titmuss' published work can be read as a continuous indictment of the values of private enterprise and the profit motive. It is therefore easier for us to form an impression of the kind of economic system which he would have eschewed than to identify the one which he preferred. He alludes to general entities such as 'an integrated society', providing 'universalist services outside the market on the principle of need'. We are, however, left uncertain as to the system of values and means by which goods and services are to be produced within the economic market.

The apparent direction of this approach to welfare is towards a socially administered society which carries a residual burden of capitalism, but it would be a system for the distribution rather than the production of wealth and welfare.

So long as there has remained some semblance of growth in the British economy, social administrators have been able to maintain this notion of a moral division between the ethics of the social market and those of the economic market. It has also been possible for us to remain remarkably indifferent to the likely disincentive effects of higher taxation on work incentives. There is an extensive literature demonstrating that at the lowest income levels, where the poverty trap occurs, such disincentives may be very important indeed. There is another extensive literature emphasizing the relativity of poverty and felt deprivation. There is not yet a coherent theory which brings together these areas of knowledge and then extends the enquiry into the middle and upper income ranges. Yet we may now be reaching a stage at which the backlash against social market values will gather sufficient public support to inflict lasting damage upon our statutory social services.

In his great lecture, 'The Social Division of Welfare', given in 1955 and published in 1956, Titmuss drew up an agenda for enquiry in which he seemed poised to break free from the traditional confines of social policy and administration. In one sense he did so, by defining social services in terms of their aims rather than their administrative form and location, thereby including within his compass not only the statutory social services but also the fiscal and occupational welfare services. In the end, however, he characterized their relationship in terms of division rather than unity. The model was used thereafter to justify a moral indictment of the fiscal and occupational systems of welfare: a seal was set upon the division between the ethics of work and the ethics of welfare which was to last for another twenty years.

The essence of that political debate was contained in the 'one fundamental question of equity' raised by the growth of fiscal and occupational policies, namely, 'whether and to what extent social service dependency benefits would be proportionately related to occupational and income achievement'.

The next major onslaught came six years later in Titmuss' Fabian lecture, 'The Irresponsible Society', in which he described the growth of occupational welfare schemes in Britain as evidence of the 'threatening concentration of power and privilege' and the 'contradictions which are distorting the economy and blurring the moral values of society'. Later Titmuss was to oppose Britain's entry into the Common Market on the grounds that the social values of western Germany and France were insufficiently 'compassionate and civilized in "world terms"'. His internationalism derived from his concern for the universal stranger and went beyond the regional groupings of industrial nations.

The question of internationalism brings us to the third of the problematic aspects of Titmuss' approach to social policy. I have suggested that his analytical model is based on an oversimplified distinction between egoism and altruism which fails to take into account the ambivalent nature of felt obligation stemming from familial loyalties. It also encourages us to underestimate the fact that there are citizens who believe that the workings of the economic market do ensure in large part a just allocation of life's material rewards. If we believe that most people accord the highest priority to their familial interests, it is difficult to see how Titmuss' social market is to achieve ultimate ascendancy, both moral and political, over the economic market. He looked to democratic processes in general and fiscal policies in particular as the means to that end, but what would be the economic costs of such a transformation? Would a society governed by the values of the social market ever become as affluent as it might have done as an acquisitive society, and would its citizens be any more

Nat into - Poortrich

altruistic when it came to setting the interests of poorer societies against their own national interests?

In his own work Titmuss was not unmindful of national interests. Indeed it was his overriding concern that national interests should include the poor as well as the rich. Given his insistence on the moral pre-eminence of international welfare, however, it is both easy to overlook that element in his work and difficult to apply certain parts of his analytical model in the real world, because the model is really a prescription for a better world as well as a better Britain.

It is when we consider Titmuss' first and last major contributions that we can most easily bring together in one framework the shifting emphases of his philosophical concerns. *Problems of Social Policy* is still his masterpiece. This study of the development of the British social services during the Second World War is dominated by the themes of family and community. The attachment of ordinary people to their kin and neighbourhoods comes through as a major reason why civilian morale survived the terrors, disorganizations and deprivations of modern warfare. Familial and communal loyalties provided the necessary 'reserves of strength and moral power' and sustained the individual's sense of purpose and self-respect in adversity. As Titmuss observes, 'A stable society rests on the basis of family life. A threat to society implies a threat to the family.' The national response grew outwards from these countless families and communities, sustained by 'the warmhearted impulse of people for a more generous society'.

The Gift Relationship seeks to convince us that the range of these generous sentiments can be extended from family and neighbourhood, beyond national frontiers, to encompass the universal stranger. The question remains, however, not as to whether the thesis holds good with regard to the unique example of blood donorship but whether it can be sustained with regard to other, more costly gifts in contexts other than the adversities of war and at the level of sovereign states rather than particular social services.

At the beginning of this century increasing public concern about national efficiency stimulated many long overdue and much needed social reforms. Forty years later Beveridge, the last of the great Edwardian social reformers, used his report to demonstrate the connections between patriotism and social reform. In *Problems of Social Policy* Titmuss wrote about a period in which British society seemed to be discovering the welfare values and aims which he most esteemed. The shared adversities of war strengthened our collective determination that thenceforward all compatriots would enjoy the benefits of a

more just and compassionate welfare system. The time and the prospects were such that Titmuss, writing in the late 1940s, was able to
take a whole society to illustrate his thesis regarding the integrative role
of social welfare.

The Gift Relationship was a reaffirmation of the values which he
still believed to be capable and worthy of universal adoption, but the
illustrative example had narrowed from a whole society to a special
sector of medical care. Britain had not become the kind of welfare
society which he had always envisaged. Titmuss' antipathy to the
values of the competitive economic market, expressed in his attacks on
occupational welfare and his condemnation of the Common Market,
remained to the end.

In certain passages of Problems of Social Policy Titmuss's empathy
with actual times and places is so intense that we are made to feel, as
Eliot once wrote, that 'History is now and England'. The integration
of familial, communal and national welfare interests was an ideal ap-
proaching its realization. By contrast the moral sentiments expressed
in The Gift Relationship are so idealistic that, although they may find
a place in the exotic customs of certain tribal societies or in a particular sector of social policy in contemporary Britain, they have no
country. In this, as he did in the postscript to Social Policy, Titmuss
finds his welfare ideals exemplified by the values and practices of the
British National Health Service ('the most unsordid act of British social
policy in the twentieth century') rather than the total society of which
it is a part. The range of societal coverage has been narrowed to what
might be described as a residual institution of the halcyon years of
post-war collectivism.

In Problems of Social Policy Titmuss convincingly demonstrates the
integrative processes which hold families, localities and nations together.
In The Gift Relationship he explores the nature of giving and receiving
between individuals rather than between nations. The approach is
psychological rather than sociological, except in the sections of the
book which so strikingly illustrate the extent to which the richest
nations actually take scarce resources away from the poorer ones.
Wartime Britain came nearest to demonstrating in practice one aspect
of Titmuss' integrative ideals, but that was a society which was united
against outside enemies. It does not follow that those ideals can be
extended from a national to an international context simply through
the subordination of the values of the economic market to those of the
social market. Unfortunately, as Titmuss himself observed, there is
little convincing evidence that even under conditions of economic

growth rich nations are disposed to share significantly more of their increased wealth with poor nations. There is, however, some evidence that in times of economic crisis and decline this disposition to give is greatly weakened. When the adversities of unemployment and inflation engender a new sense of national consciousness, it is of a kind which tends to be inward- rather than outward-looking.

The relationship between national and international forms of altruism rests on a delicate balance of potentially conflicting values. Charity necessarily begins at home, because that is where it is best learned. A nation of compatriots who do not think well of themselves as a nation and who neglect their own poor is unlikely to deal compassionately with universal strangers. At the same time a too powerful assertion of national interests can be swiftly destructive of international welfare.

Social administration carried a heavy load of human longing for a better world. The promise of social justice is part of the perennial attraction of Marxism, but injunctions to unconditional altruism continue also to be a powerful element in the work of many non-Marxist social administrators. This tradition is exemplified in the work of Titmuss. In the general intellectual climate of Britain today internationalism is self-evidently respectable and patriotism is not. Overt Patriotism, provided that it goes under the name of 'nationalism', tends to be viewed as a virtue only when it is practised by universal strangers. We would do well, however, to note William Letwin's suggestion that in the bestowal of his affection and benevolence the ordinary citizen 'naturally concentrates on a selected number of persons who are closest to him in the moral sense, his family, old friends, neighbours and compatriots, in descending order'. *Problems of Social Policy* provides some powerful evidence in support of this assertion. *The Gift Relationship* does not have a sufficiently extensive societal grounding to convince us that this order of affective priorities can be either modified or extended in the real world to encompass the international community.

This is not to deny that the claims of the universal stranger have some authority but to point that they are a part of a complex network of claims and entitlements. Even if we were to make unconditional altruism the crowning glory of our moral sentiments, it would be as well for us to remember that crowns are reserved for special occasions and that most good deeds are done in the fustian of a more homespun philosophy. The really difficult moral problems in social welfare arise for us not when we are establishing the superordinate authority of one claim over all others but when we are working out the criteria by which we can reconcile many conflicting claims, each of

competing claims ↑

which has an equal right to consideration. On what grounds, for example, can relatively affluent altruists in Britain justify the dispensation of taxpayers' money for overseas aid, so long as poverty persists in their own country? How 'powerless' do the poor feel in the face of such implacable altruism? In a nation which had already fulfilled the Titmussian criteria for a welfare society, it would not be necessary to ask questions such as these, but they must be faced, now that the consciousness of relative poverty is becoming more widespread, as our economic crisis deepens.

These questions which I have raised differ in emphasis from those of Reisman especially with regard to *The Gift Relationship*. They also imply a different kind of political expectation from that which can be inferred from Titmuss' later work. Were I able to share the optimism about human nature and the future of collectivist social policies which seemed to inspire Titmuss to the end, I would find *The Gift Relationship* a more convincing work.

Social administration owes an incalculable debt to Richard Titmuss. The questions which he posed about value and choice still have relevance today, but his answers must be subjected to a continuous reappraisal, if we are not to render him the disservice of converting into doctrinal orthodoxy his most innovative contribution.

David Reisman enters this debate with the advantage of not being a social administrator. He has consequently brought a fresh perspective and perhaps a measure of detachment less easily achieved by those of us who grew up within the subject. He argues, for example, that Titmuss neglected in general terms the field of 'economic welfare' and in particular those of employment policy and economic planning. He has much of interest to say about Titmuss' apparent reluctance to develop a theory of values which might have carried his analysis of altruism beyond a prescriptive level. In exploring this issue, David Reisman points to Titmuss' highly normative treatment of the phenomenon of stigma in social policy and its association with selectivity.

This is a book which will also cause many social administrators to reflect again about the collectivist assumptions which underpin much contemporary thinking about social welfare. Its author questions the extent to which collectivist values can ever become a dominant influence in capitalist societies. He reminds us that the residualist model of social welfare is based upon a defensible set of moral principles and that some citizens are as likely to feel stigmatized by the operations of the social market as by those of the economic market. In examining such topics Reisman goes on to argue that Titmuss' theory of social causation is inadequate partly because it undervalues the factor of individual responsibility and overemphasizes the consequences of 'unidentifiable causality'.

In practical terms, David Reisman restates the case for user-charges, and other methods such as the use of vouchers which might increase choice in the public sector. These were not policies favoured by Titmuss during his lifetime.

Titmuss was a man of prodigious energy and his capacity for sustained hard work was legendary. The range and quality of his academic output becomes all the more impressive when account is taken of his continuous record of public service. Yet it is always the ironic fate of truly original thinkers like Titmuss that those who follow them regret that they did not find time to write more about the issues they were the first to explore. As Reisman implies, no writer was better qualified to develop a general theory of welfare than Titmuss because it was he more than anyone else who made such an advance both possible and necessary. We can still speculate about the form which such a theory might have taken although we know that Titmuss was suspicious of all such intellectual enterprises.

At the end of his book Reisman concludes that 'Titmuss' system is the best we have' and that his outstanding contribution to the study of the welfare state rests upon the manner in which he developed a philosophy of welfare, the principles of which remained grounded in a meticulous regard for empirical evidence. Secondly, he gave a coherent sociological dimension to the study of social policy and did more than anyone else in his time to renew the traditions of a sociology of relevance. Thirdly, he wrote with elegance, clarity and wit and thereby secured for his subject a readership amongst the general public.

Reisman also reminds us of the close theoretical and philosophical affinities which Titmuss had with Durkheim and Weber. Each of these great men addressed himself to the fundamental social problems of his time. All three were deeply imbued with and inspired by a compassion for their fellows and a commitment to enhancing the quality of social life and the elimination of injustice. Like Durkheim's and Weber's, Titmuss' reputation as one of the great innovators in the social sciences will survive and grow. His achievements will be the subject of continuous review and reappraisal. David Reisman's book is greatly to be welcomed as one of the first contributions to that debate and as an exciting and original work in its own right.

Robert Pinker

Greenwich, July 1977

1 Introduction

Richard Morris Titmuss was appointed Professor of Social Administration at the London School of Economics in 1950. He was not the architect of the modern British welfare state, but he soon made himself its ideologue, although as much its critic as its advocate. His ideas can be traced back to his influential essay, 'The Social Division of Welfare' (1956), and the general consistency of outlook in the years that followed is remarkable. His main works are *Problems of Social Policy* (1950), *Essays on 'The Welfare State'* (1958), *Income Distribution and Social Change* (1962), *Commitment to Welfare* (1968), *The Gift Relationship* (1970), and *Social Policy* (1974). The latter is a posthumously published version of the lecture notes he used in the University of London. In addition, he was also co-author of three influential studies of more specialized interest: *The Cost of the National Health Service in England and Wales* (1956) (with Brian Abel-Smith), *Social Policies and Population Growth in Mauritius* (1961) (with Brian Abel-Smith and Tony Lynes), and *The Health Services of Tanganyika* (1964) (with Brian Abel-Smith, George Macdonald, Arthur Williams and Christopher Ward).

Titmuss was an original, creative, sensitive and influential thinker, whose work unfortunately does not always win the understanding it deserves. Titmuss is a difficult author, partly because he was more addicted to writing essays than books (even his books tend to be long essays or collections of essays), and partly because he never saw the need to make his underlying intellectual system fully explicit. One purpose of the present study is to reconstruct that system, to re-assemble the pieces of the puzzle, and thus to demonstrate that the Titmussian world is a unified whole made one by his sincere attempt to restore the study of welfare to its proper place in the study of society. A second purpose of the present study is to evaluate the system and to note its essential paradox: Titmuss stressed integration most (whether of human knowledge or of man in society) but left his own model incomplete and unintegrated. To some extent, however, such imprecision is bound to be the fate of all those who attempt a science of society. It is not only for himself that Titmuss was speaking when he confessed: 'The more I try to understand the role of welfare and the human condition the more untidy it all becomes.'[1]

Richard Titmuss was born on 16th October 1907, the son of a Bedfordshire small farmer. He left school at 15 and, after a job as an office boy in Standard Telephones, entered the County Fire Insurance Office at the age of 18. It was also at that time that he became the family breadwinner and came to understand at first hand the burden of dependency: his mother, who had married young and never fully reconciled herself to the fact that her husband was only a small farmer, was both financially and emotionally dependent on him until her death in February 1972. The financial burden was slightly eased when she won a football pool after the Second World War, however.

Within the insurance company, Titmuss rose rapidly to become a London Inspector at the early age of 32. He learned about the dependent both as statistics and as case histories, and also acquired an insight into the way in which institutional investors deploy their funds. Moreover, when he finally left County Life in 1942, he personally experienced the exercise of power without responsibility through the loss of sixteen years of occupational pension rights.

Meanwhile, Titmuss married Kay Miller in 1937 when he was 30 and she was 35. She had worked in London clubs for the unemployed and was to a large extent responsible for developing his interest in social and political questions. In the preface to his first book, Titmuss declared: 'It is my wife, Kay – not only by her part in the publication of this book, but through her work among the unemployed and forgotten men and women of London – who has helped me to visualise the human significance, and often the human tragedy, hidden behind each fact.'[2] Throughout their life together, Kay was a source of strength and understanding. As Margaret Gowing says in her valuable essay on Titmuss: 'He could support the great weight of work and maintain his inner calm because of his happiness at home with Kay. Looking after Richard was her life work.'[3] They had one daughter, Ann, who was born in 1944 and, not surprisingly, became a sociologist.

In the late 1930s, Titmuss began to write articles and books on social questions such as migration, poverty, stratification and public health. *Poverty and Population* (published in 1938) was an essay on social waste which demonstrated the association between sickness and death on the one hand, and malnutrition and low incomes on the other. *Our Food Problem* (written with a friend, F. Le Gros Clark and published in 1939) continued the discussion on malnutrition and proved both influential and controversial: some 30,000 copies were sold before the outbreak of war. Then came *Parents Revolt* (1942), a book on family planning written with Kay Titmuss and containing a foreword by Beatrice Webb; and *Birth, Poverty and Wealth* (1943), which dealt with infant mortality. There he showed that the difference in infant death-rates between the most and the least privileged social classes was greater in 1930–2 than it had been twenty years earlier; and argued that if all classes had had the same infant death-rates in 1930–2 as Class I, then 90,000 lives would have been spared.

These early works show a scrupulous attention to detail and a strong commitment to impartial scientific investigation. It was in this period that Titmuss became a Fellow of the Royal Statistical Society and the Royal Economic Society, and also received money for research from the Leverhulme Trust. These early works demonstrate too an increasing interest in the socio-economic origins of poverty and in the relationship between inequality and dependency; so it is no surprise that Titmuss switched his allegiance at about the same time from the Liberal to the Labour Party (a much more radical choice then than it would be today).

In 1939 Titmuss was deferred from conscription because of his post in insurance (where he had become involved in war damage insurance). The war nonetheless had a deep influence on him. For one thing, just as the Depression had shown how social forces could generate vast unrelieved states of dependency, so the war proved that men in society could work together in pursuit of a common aim. Moreover, he was in 1942 invited by Keith (later Sir Keith) Hancock to join the team of historians who were writing the civil history of the war. Titmuss was to be concerned with social services (ranging from the evacuation and billeting of mothers and children to health, social security, and care of the homeless), a project which occupied him until 1949. His contribution to the series, *Problems of Social Policy*, was published in 1950. In it he showed mastery of vast quantities of material (some of it published, but most of it collected directly from government departments and a wide range of welfare institutions) and also sensitivity to moral dilemmas, value choices and human problems. R. H. Tawney regarded it as little short of brilliant: 'Sociology, like history, is a department of knowledge which requires that facts should be counted and weighed, but which, if it omits to make allowance for the imponderables, is unlikely to weigh or even to count them right. Mr. Titmus is a humane scientist who does not succumb to the temptation to "measure the universe by rule and line." His subtlety and insight in interpreting his evidence are as impressive as the meticulous scrupulousness with which he has collected and sifted it.'[4]

Problems of Social Policy showed insight and was exceptionally well written. It ultimately sold more copies than any other volume in the series and led, together with Hancock's enthusiastic recommendation, to Titmuss being appointed in 1950 to the new Chair of Social Administration at the London School of Economics. It was Titmuss' first academic post (which meant he had never had to conform to the rigidity of departmental conventional wisdom to win appointment or promotion). He had no university degree (although he eventually received five honorary doctorates and numerous other honours, such as the C.B.E. and election to the British Academy) nor, indeed, even the equivalent of a school-leaving certificate.

The London School of Economics in 1950, although part of the University of London, had no natural scientists and few arts staff. It was almost entirely a social science college, and the resultant continuous and stimulating debate on social issues was valuable to the new, largely self-educated professor. Titmuss was also fortunate in inheriting from T. H. Marshall a strong department of thirteen members. Titmuss was, of course, not a trained social worker, a fact which brought him into conflict with some of his colleagues; but this conflict was to some extent resolved by the demonstration effect of his strong commitment to vocational social work education. He also won admiration from many of his associates for the institution of reforms such as the admission of older students without formal academic qualifications.

At the London School of Economics Titmuss moulded the new subject of Social Policy and Administration, demonstrated that it could be both academically and intellectually respectable, and trained a vast number of practitioners, both British and foreign. In this way as well as through his writings he came to have a world-wide influence on discussions about welfare. Nor should one forget that many important studies in the 1950s and 1960s (quite apart from his own impressive list of publications) were done under Titmuss' supervision or subjected to his scrutiny before publication. He was never too busy to comment on or discuss the work of others; and was noteworthy for his modesty, his kindly helpfulness, his approachability and simplicity, as well as for his assiduity and dedication to his own research. It is indicative of the lack of arrogance of the man that he always refused to travel First Class on the railways, and declined a life peerage lest it isolate him from his fellow citizens. He was widely respected by students, academics and politicians, not least for his passionate commitment to welfare, social justice and social equality. It would also be true to say, however, that he was less than loved by student radicals in the troubled years of 1966–8, when Titmuss' usual tolerance temporarily failed him and he voted noisily for hierarchy and discipline.

Titmuss was more than just an academic. While the main lines of the modern British welfare state were laid down before he became influential, he acted, while a Professor at the London School of Economics, as adviser to the Labour Party on matters such as pensions, and was bitterly disappointed when its national super-annuation scheme was lost in 1970. Had the election of that year which ended six years of Labour government been called only a few months later, the Bill would have become an Act.

Outside party politics, Titmuss sat on a number of government committees, such as the National Insurance Advisory Committee, the Royal Commission on Medical Education, and the One Parent Family (Finer) Committee. He demonstrated his interest in race relations by serving on the Community Relations Commission from 1968 to 1971, and in the problem of poverty by acting as Deputy Chairman of the Supplementary Benefits Commission from 1968 to 1973. This last post is a surprise since Supplementary Benefits are means-tested, and Titmuss was a vociferous enemy of the means test. Perhaps, however, as Margaret Gowing believes, 'he saw the Commission's work as one way of exercising the positive discrimination in favour of the under-privileged which was necessary on top of universalist benefits.'[5]

Titmuss was interested in the problems of poor countries, and set up at the L.S.E. the first course in Britain in development administration. In his writings he stressed that developing countries, in their quest for economic growth, should pay due attention to social growth as well; and repeated this point in the recommendations he made to the governments of Tanzania (where he and Julius Nyerere influenced each other greatly) and Mauritius.

Richard Titmuss did not live to be 'eccentric in old age' as he had hoped. Instead, he died of cancer in a National Health hospital (the Central Middlesex) on 6th April 1973. He was 65.

Part One

THE STATUS OF SOCIAL POLICY

2 The Definition of Social Policy

All policy means choice involving change: and thus implies by its very nature that we 'believe we can affect change in some form or another. We do not have policies about the weather because, as yet, we are powerless to do anything about the weather.'[1] Yet precisely because it cannot escape the constraint of choice involving change, because it is action-oriented and problem-oriented, no policy can escape from values, ideologies and images of what constitutes the 'good society'. Hence Professor Titmuss stressed that human values simply cannot be ignored in any meaningful discussion of social policy. Since in the last analysis, 'social policy is all about social purposes and choices between them'[2], it is obvious that it can never be 'value free': 'We all have our values and our prejudices; we all have our rights and duties as citizens, and our rights and duties as teachers and students. At the very least, we have a responsibility for making our values clear; and we have a special duty to do so when we are discussing such a subject as social policy which, quite clearly, has no meaning at all if it is considered to be neutral in terms of values.'[3]

Social policy thus has its origins in the values of a particular society and 'cannot be discussed or even conceptualised in a social vacuum.'[4] Welfare systems tend to 'reflect the dominant cultural and political characteristics of their societies'[5] and must be seen 'in the context of a particular set of circumstances, a given society and culture, and a more or less specified period of historical time.'[6] Social policy, in short, is social because and where needs are defined to be social: 'All collectively provided services are deliberately designed to meet certain socially recognized "needs"; they are manifestations, first, of society's will to survive as an organic whole and, second, of the expressed wish of all the people to assist the survival of some people.'[7]

There are two points to note here:

First, social policy is concerned with those needs which must be satisfied if the existing social matrix is to continue in existence. It is thus group policy not just in its origins but in its functions as well, since it has a deeply integrative and communitarian objective. Hence the primary areas of unifying interest for social policy 'are centred in those social institutions that foster integration and discourage alienation.'[8] Its model is the gift or unilateral transfer rather than the exchange of equivalents or the *quid pro quo*. Professor Titmuss believed that social policy is 'profoundly concerned with questions of personal identity whereas economic policy centres round exchange or bilateral transfer.'[9] and went still further to assert that, save in terms of its aims, objectives and ends, there is no consistent definition of social policy.[10] It is not, in short, particular institutions themselves that make up social welfare but their functions within the social structure: 'The definition, for most purposes, of what is a "social service" should take its stand on aims, not on the administrative methods and institutional devices employed to achieve them.'[11]

Second, social policy is concerned with those states of dependency which are generally recognized by the collectivity to be collective responsibilities: 'These "states of dependency" arise for the vast majority of the population whenever they are not in a position to "earn life" for themselves and their families; they are then dependent people.'[12] The reasons for the dependency might be related to the life cycle (as in the case of the very young or the very old), the mind (as in the case of the psychologically ill), the economy (as in the case of unemployment created by regional policies), and the dependent person might not indeed even recognize all the social needs that are being met. An urban black, for example, might desire medical attention which has the manifest function of making him well, and yet find that care in an integrated ward where the same universalist benefits are available to all will also make him happily integrated, a latent function he did not anticipate. Such integration is an example of a benefit to the community in its own right, and is conceptually independent of any benefits that may accrue to the individual. Other social needs affecting the community as a whole might be for the probation services, law and order, or the prevention of infectious diseases; and the case for equality itself, in Titmuss' view, comes into this category. The justification for equality is to be sought in 'the will of society to move towards a more equal society', and its extent is to be governed by the rule 'to each according to *our needs*'[13] (rather than according to the needs, work, merit or worth of the individual).

Both points that we have just considered remind us that the amount and nature of assistance offered under the heading of social policy depend 'on prevailing notions of what constitutes a "need"'[14] (and on how far the group as a whole is held responsible for satisfying it). Historically and comparatively, 'no consistent principle seems to obtain in the definition of what is a "social service"'.[15] For modern Britain, however, we may induce the following from experience: in modern Britain the discipline called 'Social Policy and Administration' is concerned with identifying social needs and with the structure of administration necessary to satisfy them. It studies the nature and distribution of social benefits and social costs; the rights and duties of the citizen both as contributor to and consumer of the social services; the interaction between the three systems of welfare that constitute collective intervention to meet selected needs (social welfare, occupational welfare and fiscal welfare); and the command-over-resources-over-time. It identifies the present-day social services as involving state education, local authority housing, social security, the National Health Service (in both its preventive and its curative functions), and other directly administered services and transfer payments. The benefits can be in cash (e.g. old-age pensions or unemployment benefits) or in kind (e.g. hospital services), but in all cases government and not the economic market is the allocating agent for rights, duties and collective consumption and the objectives are wherever possible emerging as the following: 'Social policy in Britain in the personal health, welfare and education fields is moving toward integrated community services, preventive in outlook and of high quality for all citizens in all areas irrespective of means, social class, occupation or ethnic group.'[16]

This is the state of affairs in modern Britain. Yet, because values and priorities are pre-eminently social facts, it is understandable that the scope for collective provision is elastic and that the role of social policy in practical terms varies from period to period and place to place.

Consider first variation over time in the sort of policies that should be 'social', and here Titmuss records a change both in the underlying nature of social reality and in popular attitudes: 'The Britain of the 1950s is a very different society from the Britain of the 1900s. Not only are the "needs" and "situations" different but they are differently seen.'[17] Naturally, ideas go deep into the past (witness the vestigial influence of the Poor Laws, for example, or of the crude utilitarianism of Economic Man), and in that sense 'reality starts with history.'[18]

Yet, despite the fact that 'we all drag about with us the chains of history,'[19] changes in phenomena and perception do take place. Such changes in the field of welfare have been brought about by both intellectual and material forces. As an example of the former we may consider the influence of Marx, Freud or democratic socialists such as Tawney. As an example of the latter, we may take the technological revolution or the revolution of rising expectations. As is well known, 'rising standards of living and of education have shifted the emphasis in social services from quantity to quality.'[20] This process has been accelerated by the inclusion of the middle classes in the welfare state, stridently demanding services of the standard to which they would like to be accustomed and thereby generating a bonus for the lower classes. This illustrates how our definitions of adequacy and our priorities are still in a process of evolution and are shaped by social factors.

Titmuss believed that social thinking on matters of welfare in the twentieth century had also been considerably influenced by war. In the Second World War, for example, the evacuation of mothers and children led to reports of lice, skin diseases, undernourishment, poor clothing, and exposed the extent of bad housing and poverty: 'The shock to public opinion over the condition of some of the evacuees rivalled the outcry after the Boer War with its disclosures of sickness and low physical standards.'[21] Again, the co-operation of the masses and social integration in wartime are only possible if marked differences in the population (say, in the ability to afford luxury entertainment) are reduced: 'The waging of modern war presupposes and imposes a great increase in social discipline; moreover, this discipline is only tolerable if – and only if – social inequalities are not intolerable.'[22] Then, too, war shifted the emphasis away from 'a philosophy which regarded individual distress as a mark of social incapacity'[23] and towards a more altruistic approach according to which *new* forms of assistance were to be offered without social discrimination to *all* groups in the population on the basis of 'the pooling of national resources and the sharing of risks.'[24] Hitler's bombs succeeded where the Depression of the 1930s had failed, in imposing a *de facto* structure of universalism on a multitude of welfare benefits. After all, the diswelfare costs were demonstrably universal as well: 'That all were engaged in war whereas only some were afflicted with poverty and disease had much to do with the less constraining, less discriminating scope and quality of the war-time social services. Damage to homes and injuries to persons were not less likely among the rich than the poor.'[25] Nor, incidentally, was the need for adequate widow's pensions or the use of rehabilitation centres. This presumably too meant greater tolerance by the rich of adequate rent subsidies for the poor, since such subsidies covered the same sort of socially imposed costs as the benefits which the rich themselves had begun to receive.

Such tolerance was further stimulated by the highly desirable sense of community that came about as a result of wartime setbacks, bombing, and a clearly defined sense of common purpose. Titmuss, like many others of his generation, welcomed the changes in social values and social policy that were induced by the spirit of Dunkirk. He argues that in the summer of 1940 'the mood of the people changed and, in sympathetic response, values changed as well. If dangers were to be shared, then resources should also be shared.'[26] Dunkirk was a milestone in the history of the social services since it unleashed a flood of critical debate and national introspection, and caused even *The Times* to call in a leader for greater social organization, better economic planning, and more equitable conditions of income distribution. In July 1940 the Treasury took steps to increase the number and quality of school meals and to ensure that more milk be provided for expectant and nursing mothers and young children. It is interesting that this decision was taken only five days after the Dunkirk evacuation,[27] and that these early steps were followed by numerous other measures (such as the provision of cheap or free supplies of orange juice and cod-liver oil; or a nationwide campaign to immunize children against diphtheria). All of this is evidence to support Titmuss' view on the Dunkirk evacuation: 'The long, dispiriting years of hard work that followed these dramatic events on the home front served only to reinforce the war-warmed impulse of people for a more generous society.'[28] The Second World War was thus immediately responsible for the Beveridge Report of 1942, the Education Act of 1944 and probably also the creation of the National Health Service in 1946.

Titmuss, like Tawney, had a 'historian's eye to the future'[29] and was convinced he had learnt the following vital lesson from Britain's wartime experience: people, once aware of the common situation which they share with their fellow citizens, will opt for non-discriminatory benefits available to all members of the crew, services which will moreover themselves increase still further the sense of belonging and integration. In this way the sense of social duty, the perception of common humanity and the awareness of citizenship rights become cumulative over time; and are in turn fostered by the atmosphere of planning that results.

We have been considering variations over time in the sort of policies that are regarded as being properly 'social'. It will be useful now to consider variations from place to place. There is, after all, no absolute definition of what constitutes a social 'need' independent of those standards that are shaped by a given society; and the use of the comparative method reveals important differences in attitudes from one culture to another.

Titmuss rejected those theories common in the 1950s and 1960s which postulated the death of ideology (in a world increasingly based on economic and technological rationality) and the imminence of convergence as between advanced industrial societies (due to similarities in technology and the exploitation of mass-consumption markets). The fact is that countries are not tending to become more and more alike 'in terms of their dominant value systems and political ideologies', as Titmuss' own study of paid and unpaid blood donorship indicates: 'This study throws doubt on such theories. There is no indication of convergence over the last twenty years in the pattern of blood donor gift-relationships when comparisons are made between the United States and Britain.'[30]

Blood-donorship patterns may be regarded as a useful index of social beliefs and values; and hence Titmuss uses an eight-point scale ranging from the paid donor at one extreme (motivated solely by the promise of cash-compensation) to the voluntary community donor at the other (motivated by the altruistic desire to give to strangers regardless of what he gets in return) to make comparisons in attitudes and ideas between societies. His conclusions are unambiguous: 'Different social and political structures and value systems strongly determine the typology distributions.'[31] The differences between, say, Britain, Russia, the United States and Japan in blood-donorship patterns 'cannot be explained simply in terms of administrative and organizational structures of blood supply systems and patterns of medical care services. The causal factors are more fundamental than that; ultimately, explanations – and, admittedly, explanations can never be more than partial – have to be sought in the history, the values and the political ideas of each society.'[32]

The fact that there is not a unique developmental path to which all countries must willy nilly conform is a source of freedom: 'The sense of freedom and self-respect, implicit in the notion of purposive control over man's secular affairs, can be diminished if it is believed that political choice has been narrowed to considerations of technique and administration.'[33] Where there are no radical choices to be made, 'political democracy becomes a device for choosing between different leaders but not between different social objectives,'[34] and man's ability to shape his own future is diminished. The end of ideology is hence a most lamentable state of affairs since it reduces the range of choices open to a country to express its unique value orientation, or to change its institutions as that value orientation alters.

Were ideology to drop out of the social welfare equation, the social policy-maker would be left with techniques but not values. Yet, since 'policy, any policy, to be effective must choose an objective and must face dilemmas of choice,'[35] he is bound to feel confused without an ideological map capable of focusing his attention. Thus, 'social policy models .... with all their apparent remoteness from reality, can serve a purpose in providing us with an ideological framework which may stimulate us to ask the significant questions and to expose the significant choices.'[36] Social policy presupposes social choices which presuppose social values, and must evolve from widely held attitudes rather than be imposed from above by a power élite. Societies, like individuals, must make choices, and in a democracy these choices must be made collectively.

Suppose, for example, that the decision-maker is confronted with a choice between equity and equality, between selectivity and universalism, between cost-effectiveness and social justice, between individual liberty and collective responsibility, or between the principle of charity and that of compensation. Suppose, in a concrete case, that he must decide whether an income maintenance scheme should be associated with compulsory retraining and rehabilitation (or, alternatively, be extended indefinitely to a consumer who refuses to mend his way of life); or whether poor parents should receive cash supplementation (rather than payments in kind or tied to specific purposes such as schooling or transport); or whether to means-test applicants for Supplementary Benefits (instead of providing these benefits as of right). In all of these cases science provides no more than a spectrum of choices and a unique answer can only be found by consulting the social matrix. The solution then depends 'on the relative importance we accord to economic growth and social growth, and on how the scales are weighed between the rights of the individual and the rights of society.'[37] Even the allocation of scare resources by the market mechanism, to be legitimate, must be legitimated by social choice; and thus it is eminently plausible that the market will on occasion be rejected in favour of other social mechanisms of allocation, either because it undermines social integration or because it simply fails to meet 'publicly acknowledged needs.'[38]

Social policy, as we have seen, is conservative in nature insofar as it is concerned with those needs which must be satisfied if the existing social matrix is to continue in existence. Yet it is also radical because of the wide range of choices (choices concerning both ends and means) that is open to a society in the shaping of its own future. Professor Titmuss believed that social policy ought to be active rather than passive, and must be the instrument of a 'modern democratic society' in achieving its collective goals. Thus he wrote that 'social security has to be seen as an agent of structural change; not as a system reflecting and legitimating the *status quo.*'[39] A good example of the active social engineering role that Titmuss envisaged for social welfare policies may be found in the advice he gave to the Government of Mauritius.

The problem in Mauritius was an alarmingly rapid rise in population after the Second World War, caused by a sudden fall in mortality rates (following the virtual eradication of malaria and tuberculosis) and by an extremely high birth-rate. The latter was a social fact due partly to the low status of women (who married young since they were not expected to take jobs nor found it easy to obtain them) and partly to the social insurance function of a large family. The result of the rise in population was unemployment, under-employment, pressure on state services such as education, and falling standards of living (measured in terms of Gross National Product per capita). When Titmuss went to Mauritius in 1960, the country had one of the most rapidly expanding populations in the world and work opportunities were simply not increasing at the same rate as the number of potential workers.

Naturally Titmuss could not recommend an increase in mortality rates; and an increase in jobs, while desirable, was both a long-term measure and inadequate by itself if the population continued to increase so rapidly. Hence Titmuss' solution was to reduce birth-rates, and his proposals fall into two groups:

Firstly, he called for voluntary birth-control and recommended a nation-wide campaign to provide free facilities and information, as an integral part of health and welfare services, to all requiring assistance. He advised that every cinema and newspaper should include an advertisement at least once a week stressing the benefits of the three-child family and bringing out the fact that family planning is essential for social progress. Showing considerable tolerance, however, he recognized the validity of religious objections to contraception and advised that the new services should be neither compulsory nor prohibited: 'The right of any individual on religious or any other ground to refuse to use these services or any particular method of family limitation must be safeguarded. The right of those who wish to know and who wish to use the services must equally be upheld. The tolerances and courtesies of a liberal society must be practised by all. The illiberalities of some must not thrive on the courtesies of others.'[40] In their report to the Government of Tanganyika four years later he and his colleagues adopted an identical position. The state, they recommended, should help disseminate information about family planning (thereby giving the citizenry a legitimate choice by showing them how far births can be controlled), but it should not make the small family compulsory: 'It is for the people of Tanganyika to say whether they would prefer to have fewer and stronger children than larger numbers of undersized and sickly children.... These are questions which parents must decide. They cannot be the subject of legislation or any form of regulation.'[41]

Secondly, Titmuss proposed the creative manipulation of the pattern of social benefits to help bring about an immediate change-over to the small-sized three-child family system he regarded as so indispensable. Thus he recommended, for example, that there should be a 'Small Family Pension Benefit' of an extra 15 Rupees a month, payable to a woman of 65 or over who had given birth to not more than three live-born children and thus helped to solve the community's main social problem (the proviso being that she was still married at age 65 and had married before she was 45).[42] Again, a maternity benefit was to be provided to no woman who had borne a child (living or dead) within the 24 months previous to the expected date of the birth for which she was claiming. This would encourage the spacing of children. And other social aims were to be built into the benefit as well: thus no woman, for example, was to receive maternity benefit if she was under 21 (to encourage a later start to families), or if she already had three living children (to keep down the size of families), or if her husband had in the previous year been assessed for income tax (to skew the benefits towards the poor), or if she could not prove she had access to information on family planning at an ante-natal clinic (even if she did not in fact make use of contraceptive techniques).[43]

Similarly, Titmuss recommended a system of family allowances also aimed at discouraging the large family. A benefit of 15 Rupees per month was to be paid to each family with three dependent children under the age of 14, but there was to be no increase in benefit if the family had more than three children and no payment at all if there were fewer than three (the idea being that, in the absence of financial aid for their first or second child, parents would postpone starting a family until later when they were richer).[44] The system was to be non-contributory (so as to reach even the poorest members of the community) and was to replace tax allowances for children via the income tax system (which, because income taxes in Mauritius were progressive, benefited the rich more than the poor).[45]

Titmuss went still further in harnessing social welfare in the service of society. He recommended that a non-contributory benefit of 50 Rupees should on the occasion of a marriage be paid to the father of the bride where both bride and groom were 21 years of age or older and provided the woman had had no previous children;[46] and that the minimum age for marriage should for women be raised from 15 to 18.[47] Both measures would encourage later marriage and reduce the child-bearing period.

At the same time Mauritian doctors should be induced to work in Mauritius. Here again the welfare state could help. Scholarships should, Titmuss advised, be awarded increasingly for Mauritians to study in countries like Australia rather than Britain or France, for the simple reason that they are less likely to settle permanently in Australia.[48] Similarly, a definite quota of scholarships for study abroad should be reserved for women: quite apart from improving career prospects for women, such a stratagem would help to increase the pool of professionals on the island, since women students are more likely than their male counterparts to return home after qualifying.[49] In this way too, social welfare had an active role to play in helping to mould and structure the nature of Mauritian society.

It was because he believed that the 'integrated community services' of the modern welfare state should be active rather than passive that Professor Titmuss opposed those thinkers in Britain and the United States who he felt were fighting a rearguard action against collective progress by arguing for the reprivatization of welfare services. His reasoning was that, if the expansion of social services has a positive influence on the national health, then their contraction and their replacement by private provision is bound to have a negative influence.

Consider, for example, the move 'to set people free from the conscience of obligation'[50] by establishing private markets for blood, eyes, kidneys and other human tissues and organs (while still accepting that a market to buy and sell the whole living human being is immoral). This movement is dangerous since a substantial social cost arises whenever voluntary gifts are replaced by commercialism: 'It is likely that a decline in the spirit of altruism in one sphere of human activities will be accompanied by similar changes in attitudes, motives and relationships in other spheres.'[51] Clearly, 'if dollars or pounds exchange for blood then it may be morally acceptable for a myriad of other human activities and relationships also to exchange for dollars or pounds. Economists may fragment systems and values; other people do not.'[52]

The observer of the social scene must be sensitized to its dynamic as well as to its static properties. Specifically, he must recognize the fact that an erosion of the sense of community is likely to result from an extension of the role of market transfers in social life: 'Once man begins to say, as he sees that dollars exchange for blood supplies from Skid Row and a poor and often coloured population of sellers, "I need no longer experience (or suffer from) a sense of responsibility (or sin) in not giving to my neighbour" then the consequences are likely to be socially pervasive. There is nothing permanent about the expression of reciprocity. If the bonds of community giving are broken the result is not a state of value neutralism. The vacuum is likely to be filled by hostility and social conflict.'[53]

The ideologists of free enterprise capitalism tend to neglect the social costs that result from the narrowing of social choices to those alternatives associated with the market mechanism, and obscure the spectrum of potential choices that in fact exists. Such an attitude means that a very large number of economists in practice, and despite their oath of value neutrality, 'perform as missionaries in the social welfare field and often give the impression of possessively owning a hot line to God.'[54] Although naïve rather than malicious, such men nonetheless are dangerous once we recognize that 'the myth of maximizing economic growth can supplant the growth of social relations.'[55] The economist is insensitive to such social relations because he is imbued with an outdated methodological individualism, with abstractions lingering on from the nineteenth century and 'wrapped round the concept of individual man acting outside the matrix of his particular society.'[56]

The possessive individualism of market capitalism is unacceptable in the social welfare field. To begin with, it favours economic growth and neglects other felt needs and objectives of the social group. Yet increasingly 'we have begun to recognize that social growth – the need for integration, the need for more equality of opportunity, the need for freedom from want – deserves as much attention, intellectually as well as in terms of political action, as economic growth.'[57] Then, too, market-oriented theories stress the bilateral transfer and neglect the ethical superiority of the gift. This is the direct opposite of Professor Titmuss' own view that altruism in giving to a stranger does not begin and end with blood donations, and that as often as possible people should be put in situations where they can get in the habit of making gifts rather than writing cheques. In the last analysis, therefore, social policy is not simply about therapy for the dependent but about how people interact; and ought most of all to focus 'on processes, transactions and institutions which promote an individual's sense of identity, participation and community and allow him more freedom of choice for the expression of altruism and which, simultaneously, discourage a sense of individual alienation.'[58]

Social policy focuses on integration and involvement. So does socialism: 'Socialism is about community as well as equality. It is about what we contribute without price to the community and how we act and live as socialists.'[59] Socialism is not simply about re-distribution, about how much of the rich man's property the poor man can expect to enjoy, for 'socialism is also about giving.'[60] The fact is that the paradigm of good social policy coincides with that of the good society as conceived by the good socialist, and is the stranger-gift in blood donation. Perhaps it is true that the term social policy itself 'does not imply allegiance to any political party or ideology.'[61] It is no less true, however, that social policy as conceived of by Titmuss can hardly be divorced from socialism. Both make a value judgement stressing integration, redistribution, community and altruism and both recognize the social significance of individual needs. As Titmuss puts it, 'socialist social policies are, in my view, totally different in their purposes, philosophy and attitudes to people from Conservative social policies. They are (or should be) pre-eminently about equality, freedom and social integration.'[62] His comparison between the Labour Party's National Superannuation Bill (lost in 1970) and the Conservative's Social Security Bill led him to conclude that 'choice in this particular area of social policy is not just a matter of detail – of marginal differences in administrative organisation and social engineering. At bottom, the real choice consists of two funda-mental contrasting views of the objectives of social policy and different interpretations of the nature of man.'[63] Here as always, choice involves ideology and values. Here as always, Titmuss makes clear where his own sympathies lie.

Titmuss believed that man must continue to 'reach out for the politically impossible', and ought not simply to 'busy himself with the resurrection of utilitarian theory' or (no less deplorable) 'cultivate the new stoicism of affluence.'[64] He had reason, moreover, to be optimistic about the future. By opting in Titmuss' own time for the new welfare state, the electorate had made a value judgement in favour of social justice and the community. In such circumstances a socialist might truly be tempted to conclude that *what is* is rapidly becoming *what ought to be.*

3 Some Methodological Considerations

Social policy exists in a social context, and the social scientist cannot afford to forget that he is also a member of his society. Hence the methodological importance of four inter-related concepts: generalism, humanism, relevance, and suspicion of spurious quantification.

First, generalism. Professor Titmuss believed that 'the study of social policy cannot be isolated from the study of society as a whole in all its varied social, economic and political aspects.'[1] In discussing social policy, we simply cannot abstract from the complex changes taking place in a complex society (changes, for example, in population, the position of women or the family, social stratification, race, mobility, urbanization, industrialization, or the work ethic). Nor can we neglect the multiplicity of human needs, which make any policy discussion many-sided, multidisciplinary and interdisciplinary. Thus the discipline of Social Policy and Administration 'does not claim to be a distinctive, separate discipline'[2] or a 'self-contained specialism'.[3] Rather, it is dependent on 'the methods, techniques and insights of the historian, the economist, the statistician, the sociologist or, on occasion, some of the perspectives of the philosopher.'[4] Indeed, the subject is 'the concern of all who live in an industrial, urban country.'[5] The discipline itself has an integrative function, since it infringes 'the unwritten rules of academic trespass'[6] and is able as a result to offer the 'imaginative excitements of unifying perspectives and principles'.[7]

The student of social policy must therefore be sensitized both to the fact that social policy exists in the broader context of society itself and to the complexity of human beings. Unfortunately, the extensive and often excessive division of labour in scientific research is a force operating in the opposite direction. Nowadays many social scientists are no longer able to see the whole man: 'Industrial psychologists and sociologists .... seem to be falling into much the same trap as some economists. Hence they observe only a part and a steadily smaller part of man's life in highly industrialized societies.'[8] It is a sad fact that professionals (including the 'less gifted and less perceptive research worker'[9]) do like to retreat to some small allotment of skill and specialized knowledge where they feel secure, and it also consolidates their social status if their role and function are clearly defined and well known: we must not forget that 'professional people, whether they be doctors, social workers or teachers, are pre-eminently people with status problems.'[10] Nowadays, 'most professions ..... may sometimes be regarded as associations for spreading the gospel of self-importance.'[11] Excessive compartmentalism is an occupational hazard of excessive professionalism; and thus, at least in the social policy field, the specialist must overcome his fear of trespass and recognize the need to be to some extent a generalist.

Second, humanism. One of the reasons why Titmuss so strongly advocated generalism was his belief that a man must be seen in his fullness and richness, as an actor who plays many parts (a worker perhaps, but also a family man, a member of his community, and so on). He believed that narrow scientism and the tendency to regard people as numbers in a table were the enemy of humanism, and warned of the danger 'that concern for the value and uniqueness of the individual human being may be diminished if the scientific outlook spreads to embrace more and more of human affairs.'[12]

Titmuss recognized that statistical tools are a considerable help to the scholar as they help him to recreate human situations. He made a point, however, of looking behind the figures in order to reconstruct the real individuals who were hidden there. The following discussion of why a mother might have wanted to return from wartime evacuation to the dangers of an urban community is a good illustration of his tendency to personalize and of his sensitivity to real human beings:

There were the savings clubs and sickness associations which bound contributors to a particular voluntary hospital or firm of doctors; the well-known school treatment clinic or 'welfare' where you could get different forms of help from people who understood your trouble; the friendly society, insurance agent or co-operative, upon one of which you were relying for a small sum to buy new blankets or an extra bed; the medical officer to whom you could look for cod-liver oil for the baby, or advice about Mary's ear trouble; the health visitor – an old friend – who had done so much when Jimmy was ill and had seen him grow up and leave school; the midwife who had made arrangements for a friend to look after Jane when the last baby arrived; the lady at the Charity Organisation Society who had helped when father had all his teeth out; the school nurse, the teacher, the lady at the hospital, the assistance man and, finally, the serried ranks of check traders, secondhand dealers, hire-purchase firms and club roundsmen. These were the people who were known, liked, disliked or tolerated. They fitted into a part of life that had meaning. They were the people who helped to stop the leaks, who patched and repaired and encouraged in the cycle of birth, marriage, illness, death and all the 'rude inelegance of poverty'.[13]

In this passage Titmuss demonstrates (apart from his evident admiration for the seamless web of the working-class community) a novelist's capacity to write lyrical prose coupled with a novelist's ability to get inside the minds of other people. Nor is this passage an isolated instance. As another example of his ability to empathize with people's detailed perceptions of their own lives, consider his discussion of those unfortunate city-dwellers who 'trekked' in wartime from the towns in order to spend each night in the country: 'The fact that many people chose to trudge off into the country each evening did not, by itself, imply a deterioration in morale. These people were afraid of the bombs; of dark hours of wakefulness, of listening, sometimes tense and sometimes nodding, for the drawn-out whine, and then the rumbling murmur of a house collapsing in the blackness. Above all, they wanted sleep; for sleep was forgetfulness and rest.'[14] It is easy to dismiss such passages as cloying sentimentality. The fact remains, however, that they show that real understanding of the human condition which Titmuss envisaged as an essential complement to statistical tabulation.

Third, relevance. Social policy has the power both to observe facts and to create them as well, but the social scientist ought not to prescribe ends for the community and should accept the values it evolves. He can attempt to persuade the community that its aims are incompatible or even undesirable but must in the last analysis accept that there is a premium on social relevance and that the search for knowledge must be in the service of society.

Because of his stress on relevance, Titmuss had occasion to warn the universities that they ought not to be 'abstracted from society and wholly unresponsive to the needs of their times.'[15] 'No university can be free to establish, say, a faculty of veterinary medicine; to buy as many computers as it thinks fit; to concentrate its resources on teaching students from other countries; or to ignore completely the needs of society.'[16] Titmuss reminded the universities that they are financed by the group and must show 'responsiveness to the welfare objectives of that society.'[17] They must meet 'the trained manpower needs of their age'[18] and plan ahead to ensure that society will have adequate trained personnel with requisite skills at some date in the future. They must not forget their obligation 'to serve the needs of others and society at large'[19] as well as their own staffing needs.

The output of a university are the twin products of teaching and research. In the case of teaching, a student's education ought to embody both 'practical usefulness' and 'intellectual excitement'.[20] This means, on the one hand, that education ought to help students to acquire specific skills and prepare for a socially useful career: there is a need, as Titmuss puts it, 'for education which furthers the abilities of men and women to reason and act effectively in a variety of vocational situations'.[21] It also means, on the other hand, that education ought to help students to think independently. While rejecting as élitist the claim that 'learning to think' is an end in itself, and while insisting that men must be able to act as well as reflect, Professor Titmuss nonetheless deplored the promotion through education of excessive specialization: 'Consider the growing substitution of specialization for general education. What education for democracy is there in much of the professionalized, sectionalized diet served up today to students in most universities, technical colleges, teachers' training courses and other places of instruction? Are we not, indeed, witnessing a triumph of technique over purpose? What, in fact, are we offering to a majority of the young beside material success, the social graces, vocational techniques and, in particular, professional salvation?'[22] Titmuss thus rejected cost-benefit studies made of the effects of education on the grounds that a high rate of return on training might reflect that economic progress which is purchased at the cost of social growth: 'The current obsession which sees education as capital investment for the purpose of "keeping up in the economic race" suggests that our values are being distorted.'[23] And he warned against excessive credentialism, 'the ultimate absurdity of which might be that no public gardener would be allowed to grow roses without a Ph.D. in Horticulture.'[24]

In the social policy field, education can play a vital role in helping to train humane and enlightened social workers and other personnel, and to challenge conservative attitudes and conventions which impede an improvement in service. Such improvement is not just a question of quantity of resources. It is also a question of quality of staff: 'We know now from experience in Britain that we did not abolish the spirit of the old and hated poor law by enacting new legislation in 1948. The same people – the same administrators and workers – still had to run the hospitals, public assistance offices and welfare services. They poured into the new social service bottles the old wine of discrimination and prejudice.'[25]

The second product of the university is research, and it too should be relevant to the needs of society. Research must be the servant, not the master, and must be aimed at helping man to acquire better control over his environment so that he has more freedom to develop his personality. Again, personal contact of students with lecturers is, like personal contact of patients with doctors, vital to prevent alienation; and hence lecturers should avoid a flight into research where it means the neglect of teaching. Combining these two points, it would be true to say that a lecturer who does research on non-relevant subjects and simultaneously treats his teaching as a burden is attempting to secure his *individual* self-advancement at the *expense* of the group.

In the domain of social policy, research has the important social function of helping the community to get at the facts of the social situation and thus to make intelligent choices on the basis of the evidence rather than in that intellectual darkness where myth and prejudice thrive. Titmuss had 'a strong belief that one of the purposes of the university in the modern world is to help society to make informed political choices about economic growth, about social growth and about educational growth.'[26] Hence the academic should recognize that his primary duty is to the truth, not to professional success nor even to political ideology. He cannot, of course, escape his ideology, but he ought at least to indicate where his evidence stops and his bias begins: 'Our first and last duty is to the truth. It is because I am sceptical of the claims that are sometimes made for a value-free social science that I restate this fundamental allegiance. The values that we hold should be clear to our students; the evidence on all sides should also be clear. It is part of our responsibilities to expose more clearly the value choices that confront societies in the arena of social welfare.'[27]

Social policies are likely to be more effective if they are 'grounded in a basis of fact about reality',[28] and clearly, 'social diagnosis is needed as well as individual therapy'.[29] If the dependent are to be helped, they must first be identified and information about their condition must be made available to policy-makers. Similarly, any action to deal with the distribution of income and wealth or the burden on the health services is more likely to succeed if we can avoid assertions which 'do not rest on any firm basis of fact'.[30] The welfare state has not always benefited most those whose needs are greatest, and part of the reason has been inadequate comprehension of user-patterns and latent wants: 'Only now are we coming to see that we need much sharper tools of social study and measurement; more precise social analyses of conditions, needs and the actual functioning of services; more attempts at social planning in alliance with economic planning.'[31] In short, research in social policy, like teaching, has a dual function: it is enlightening and even exhilarating in its own right insofar as it advances 'our knowledge of human behaviour in situations of change',[32] and it is socially useful insofar as it is instrumental in bringing about a change in situations.

Social policies must be formulated on the basis of facts concerning present needs and on the basis of forecasts of future problems. Titmuss was understandably critical of the lack of intellectual preparedness in Britain on the eve of the Second World War: 'No Cabinet committee maintained a continuous watch over the social services. No research was conducted into the effects of bombing on the apparatus of civilian life. No comprehensive study was made of the social consequences that might flow from the kind of war that the Government expected. Inadequate factual knowledge and an inadequate endeavour to acquire it, a deep ignorance of social relationships and a shallow interest in social research – these things were later to handicap the work of Government Departments.'[33]

Fourth, suspicion of spurious quantification. Titmuss believed, as we have seen, that the facts are, regardless of one's value-orientation, the prerequisite for reasoned argument, and warned that 'if English social history is any guide, confusion has often been the mother of complacency.'[34] He also believed, however, that the academic should recognize the limits put upon his evidence by the simple truth that in the human sciences not all variables are measurable.

The fact is that the world of social welfare does not usually lend itself to quantification: 'We cannot easily measure the effects of particular delivery systems in the satisfaction of education, medical care, child guidance, adoption procedures, cash transfer payments and so forth.'[35] It is difficult to compare the value of two years of nursery education to a three-year-old child with the benefit accruing from two years of postgraduate education to a student reading for a Ph.D.; or to know what money value to assign to a human life saved in hospital; or to estimate the costs of slum ghettoes in terms of social frustration, racial tension and felt discrimination; or to know the extent to which altruism, by diminishing alienation, reduces the incidence of dishonesty and violence in social life; or to calculate the distress caused by the maiming, death or mental breakdown of a loved one in time of war. In general terms, we may conclude that there are few quantifiable indices of costs and benefits basically qualitative in nature: 'There are few criteria of success (though there are negative ones in the form of failure) in assessing the performance of social service systems. What is, for example, success for the Director of a Social Services Department, the Manager of a Supplementary Benefits or public assistance office, a general practitioner, a probation officer, a hostel manager for homeless people or discharged manic depressives?'[36] In such cases success-indicators may be impossible to calculate and we may have no choice but to rely on the informed value judgements and professional ethic of men who are expert in the field.

Value judgements are inescapable, and hence simple fact-gathering is insufficient. Success in making husbands pay maintenance to wives, for example, could mean a data bank society and hence the failure to preserve individual privacy; and there is no scientific means of ascertaining whether the success outweighs the failure.[37] Again, while universities ought as recipients of social funds to be cost-conscious, they ought also to recognize that their objectives are social as well as economic, and hence to reject the 'narrow world of the accountant or the sillier notions of "productivity" as applied to higher education'.[38] In the last analysis, 'human welfare is an ethical concept.'[39]

In any case, a study of success and failure in social policy would be a complex exercise were it to take into account (as it should) all present and future social costs and benefits by using a generalized sociological approach. It would be necessary to know, for instance, the percentage of the cost of a patient's stay in hospital that should be assigned to teaching and research done on him (and thus what economic 'price' should be the doctor's imputed payment to the patient for the right to use him as an input); or the opportunity cost of the voluntary blood-donor's time (remembering that the data are not precise: 'For women donors the value of housewives' services cannot be measured'[40]); or the specific value of the integration and altruism that are engendered over time by universalism in place of the market. The difficulties imposed by the temporal factor should not be underestimated. A mental patient discharged may represent success for the mental hospital (since the man is now 'off the books'), but this success may also mean the demand for a place in a hostel for the single homeless, for unemployment benefits, possibly even for police services, prisons, and research to explain a subsequent increase in crime. Here, when we follow up the case, it becomes apparent that a narrow cost-benefit study of the hospital alone would ignore many highly relevant costs and benefits throughout society. It also becomes apparent that a broader cost-benefit study would be virtually impossible to carry out. It is significant that Titmuss makes no attempt to use such an approach in his study of blood-banking systems.

The social scientist must face the fact that much of our knowledge of how men live together in groups is vague, imprecise, impressionistic, collected in situational contexts which are themselves diverse, intricate and changing. The student of social policy must recognize that the mechanistic method (involving 'a questionnaire, a random sample of delinquents, and a computer'[41]) is not a substitute for the test of the intellect; and that the field of social policy offers no quantifiable indices comparable to the engineer's measurement of efficiency or the economist's estimation of managerial success in terms of profits. The student of social policy must come to see that, compared with the more prestigious natural sciences, 'we cannot so easily measure the complex sicknesses of a complex society; the prevalence of the stress diseases of modern civilization, the instabilities of family relationships or the extent of mental ill-health in the community. Difficulties of accurate measurement should not prevent us, however, from seeking to extend our knowledge of the causes at work.'[42]

4 Part One: an Evaluation

The 'imaginative excitements of unifying perspectives and principles'[1] can all too easily become a mask for hot air and lack of rigour; generalism can come to mean superficiality as well as profundity; and a shift in emphasis from the quantitative to the qualitative can as well represent a move from hard evidence to vague impressions as from the reiocentric to the anthropocentric. Specifically, while his lofty aspirations and generous humanitarianism are refreshing in their idealism, Richard Titmuss was himself not wholly innocent of the crime of woolly thinking, as four criticisms of his views on the status of social policy will indicate.

First, Titmuss nowhere clearly defines the ideal scope of the welfare sector, and is content to delimit the social services in terms of what the general public (for reasons, as it happens, never fully explained) normally recognize them to be. Yet a definition of *what ought to be* in terms of *what is* is conservative rather than radical (more orientated towards past and present *ad hoc* concerns with social work, charity and poor relief than towards major social reform), descriptive rather than analytical (a photograph of the *status quo* rather than a prescription for optimality), and, above all, vague. Titmuss never really convinces the reader that 'social administration as a subject is not a messy conglomeration of the technical *ad hoc*.'[2]

Titmuss says that human blood is not a 'trading commodity, a market good like aspirins or cars', but rather a 'service rendered by the community for the community'[3]. Since, however, he provides no analytical dividing-line between trading commodities like aspirins and cars on the one hand, and community services like blood for transfusion on the other, the reader is left with no clear idea of where the market sector ought to stop and the welfare sector commence. Confused as to the status of exchanging, the reader is bound to ask why economic theories are not relevant for the procurement and distribution of human blood but nonetheless relevant for the procurement and distribution of aspirins and cars; and why, if decision-making by professionals is so efficient in the welfare sector (as demonstrated by the usual economic indicators of quality, choice, quantity and price), it should not then mercifully be extended to those other spheres of the economy which still suffer under the harsh rule of crude economism and market competition? Confused as to the status of giving, the reader is bound to suspect that, just as Titmuss used the free gift of blood as a paradigm for good social policy, so he was using good social policy as the paradigm for an ideal socialist society; and that Titmuss shared with many others the dream of a future society based far more on gifts, far less on exchanges, than is the case in the two-sector model with which he was most explicitly concerned.

Titmuss believed that altruism was both good business and good moral philosophy in the social welfare sector. He was, however, strangely reluctant to argue for an expansion in the empire of public provision into banking and industry or even, more modestly, to embrace those close cousins of the welfare complex left stranded in the Kingdom of the Blind. He defended the availability of pay beds in state hospitals and the existence of a parallel system of private medicine; only once directly recommended the socialization of private schooling; and had nothing to say about the nationalization either of the pharmaceutical industry (despite the symbiotic links it maintains with its dominant customer, the National Health Service, links so intimate as to recall the American military-industrial complex) or of the private insurance companies (within which, Titmuss believed, managers combine maximal power with minimal social responsibility; and which in any case perpetuate social divisions in states of dependency). In the case of insurance, Titmuss was at least prepared to advocate greater public regulation of private enterprise: noting that life insurance companies in five of the original six Common Market countries are obliged by law to invest a substantial percentage of their funds in government stock, he advised that the British government take similar measures to direct such investments.[4] Otherwise, however, he accepted that the dual system in insurance (as indeed in medicine and education) was a fact of life. Yet it is surely a curious argument to define private insurance as a 'trading commodity' and state insurance as a 'service rendered by the community for the community' (analogous to the donation of blood to unnamed strangers and aid to poorer countries). The pedantic reader will object that insurance is insurance, just as blood is blood; and may even add that apparent vagueness often conceals deliberate evasiveness reflecting excessive timidity. In Titmuss' defence, however, it must be noted that his proposal was simply for the state system to be *potentially* comprehensive. A believer in persuasion and choice rather than compulsion and force, he probably argued to himself that the alienation between public and private would one day be transcended; that the dual system would ultimately become one; and that the key to *de facto* universality lay in the last analysis in the demonstration effect of that which is not only free and accessible but provides a better service as well. It must also be noted that here as elsewhere what Titmuss argued to himself he unfortunately did not argue in detail for the benefit of his reader; and that the reader, confronted here as elsewhere with the majesty of conclusions rather than the humility of step-by-step explanation, is left with a multitude of unanswered questions. Chief among these is the following: since a dual system means a dual standard, is it not a barrier to social integration that public services will often not be utilized by those citizens wealthy enough to opt for the private? It is, after all, not just the poor in a divided community who can experience the segregation of Apartheid-like structures.

If Titmuss' discussion of the dual system is deficient, his discussion of 'economic welfare' is even more so; and this is eminently regrettable in view of the fact that economic welfare is conceptually as much a part of the welfare complex as social welfare, fiscal welfare and occupational welfare. Aid to an ailing giant in a development area is as much welfare to the workers as the alternative of paying them unemployment benefits should the firm go bankrupt. So is the Beveridge commitment to full employment (about which Titmuss has little to say), or the decision to adopt a prices and incomes policy and/or to devalue rather than introduce deflationary monetary and fiscal policies that cause men to lose their jobs. Similarly, a national minimum wage may be seen as part of the welfare complex (valuable since many of the poor require state supplementation of income precisely because they are low-paid), as may subsidies to public utilities such as transport and electricity and an anti-monopoly policy to keep the private sector competitive (valuable since many of the poor have relatively fixed incomes and are thus vulnerable to rises in the cost of living). All of these forms of economic welfare imply redistribution of the national product; but Titmuss still regards them as lying beyond the confines of social policy. Economic welfare, after all, typically concerns the independent; and it would appear that to Titmuss the social policy-maker, like the philosopher, is a man who arrives *post festum*.

Because he was principally concerned with picking up the pieces of shattered people, and because of his generally high level of aggregation, Titmuss neglected microsociological forms of economic welfare that might serve for particular groups of potential dependents the same function as the more macrosociological social services. In this context one notes that equal opportunity laws and quotas might integrate women and blacks at work to at least the same extent as the mental hospital (reinforced in due course by the Supplementary Benefits Commission) integrates them once their professional frustration has taken its toll. Titmuss, of course, would have been unwilling to impose by law what he felt should evolve from consensus. Many women and blacks will still disagree and argue that the philosopher ought to be a man who arrives *ante festum*, before it is too late; and that this can only be done by helping the independent to help themselves.

Second, Titmuss argues that the British welfare state, historically speaking, bubbled up from the collective consciousness; but he nowhere provides a rigorous and adequate theory of causality with respect to perceptions and values.

Titmuss realized that welfare and economic growth are closely associated. As he puts it, 'the social services (however we define them) can no longer be considered as "things apart"; as phenomena of marginal interest, like looking out of the window on a train journey. They are part of the journey itself. They are an integral part of industrialization.'[5] Such a necessitarian view of welfare as the inevitable concomitant of the momentum inherent in matter could be defended with reference to the breakdown of the supportive role of the family and the local community in the impersonal anonymity of modern urbanized environments: in such a situation there is simply no alternative source of care for the residual poor and deprived who cannot afford to pay for private insurance and treatment. Or, again, it could be defended in terms of the inability in a complex and mobile society to identify tort-feasors, a fact which means that social costs will be left uncovered and likely unjustly to lie where they fall. Titmuss, however, ultimately rejects the theory of complementary inputs and economic determinism, the 'notion of historical inevitability',[6] on the grounds that it neglects the crucial significance of perceptions and values. Social policy, he believed, is not value-neutral, and hence he insisted that there cannot be a unique developmental path for all countries: as proof that societies have as much freedom to reject the welfare state as to select it, witness the differences in the area of social welfare between Britain and the United States. The problem is that while he stressed that there were no tendencies towards institutional convergence, he nowhere provided a systematic explanation of the source of values such as could clarify why the welfare state varies qualitatively and quantitatively from place to place and time to time.

Titmuss, as we have seen, placed considerable emphasis on the catalytic effect in Britain of war, both insofar as it engendered a significant feeling of collective solidarity (the 'spirit of Dunkirk') and insofar as it led to widespread universality in welfare services in order to absorb shock, distress and social division. British people tended to accept the 'principle of national responsibility in time of war'[7] while they would not have done so in time of peace; new services were provided; and the realization spread that social provision was a good thing. The difficulty with this theory, however, is that it does not explain why the demand for social services did not recede with the disappearance of the external threat (and as soon as the collective solidarity of a common condition once again came under attack from those divisive sentiments usually associated in Titmuss' mind with competitive market capitalism). One could, of course, bring in intellectual influences or, for that matter, the snow-ball effect of the welfare state itself in engendering feelings of community-spiritedness and integration. Alternatively, one could argue that people continued to vote for compassion, free gifts and unilateral transfers because of the terrible selfishness of the welfare ratchet: Jack becomes accustomed to getting his skilled labour from the socialized education industry, Jill gets used to rent rebates and allowances for dependent children, and both are fully aware of the vested interest they possess in the health and prosperity of the Golden Schmoo. This argument would not, as it happens, have appealed to Titmuss, who was convinced that people vote for unilateral transfers not because they experience an unbridled lust to take without giving but because they experience a sense of altruism, neighbourliness and fellowship which makes them regard their duties as highly cherished rights. It is unfortunate that Titmuss did not explain in more detail the causes of these noble sentiments, if only to help nations to follow Britain's example; for, if war truly was the catalyst in the British case, then it still remains to be explained why America had war without welfare while Sweden had welfare without war.

Third, Titmuss, while accepting that there is no inherent reason for ideologies to converge, nonetheless naïvely accepted the existence of what T. H. Marshall describes as 'a very high degree of consensus .... about the aims of the welfare services'.[8] It is, however, eminently unrealistic to expect values to concentrate around a golden mean. Nor, parenthetically, is it necessarily a sign of social well-being when conformity and compromise replace diversity and pluralism.

Titmuss speaks of 'one publicly approved standard of service'[9] as if there were only one; and in a complex and divided society this is by no means likely to be the case. In practice, consensus has a tendency to break down the more one moves from vague and general principles to concrete and practical policies. Thus there is in modern Britain no tendency towards general agreement on the merits of comprehensive over streamed education, or on the socialization of independent schooling. There is no unambiguous consensus as to whether local authority tenants should be charged economic rents, means-tested rents geared to ability to pay, or flat-rate subsidized rents that do not differentiate between equal citizens with differentiated incomes. There is no single public opinion as to whether social security should be provided for the deprived families of convicted murderers (themselves maintained at public expense) or of men on strike (whose action may cause thousands of other men to lose their livelihood and be forced into the crowded public pocket); nor as to whether housewives should be paid civil service salaries and given appropriate holidays; nor as to whether the irresponsibly large families of careless people (often of another confession and thus doubly suspect) should be bailed out of self-imposed misery; nor as to whether a woman cohabiting with a man not her husband should be denied a widow's pension.

The point is that value differences often reflect fundamental intellectual cleavage in society; and that in such cases social policy may be quite unable to reach a compromise on the basis of a unique social will, but instead may have to opt for one set of values and scrap the other. There may, for example, be value conflict between those citizens who demand free contraception and abortion as of right on the National Health Service, and those who disapprove of scarce social resources being utilized in this way: here, to choose one policy based on one morality is to alienate the sympathies of those who support the alternative policy based on an alternative morality, and the imposition on one group of another group's values is as likely to deepen social division as to foster social integration. Or again, to take a second example, there may be value conflict based on value divergence and value dichotomy in the case of mixed neighbourhoods: it is clearly impossible for Jack (a white fascist Protestant car mechanic) to live in an exclusive area and for Jill (a black socialist Catholic Professor of Social Administration) to live in the same street in a more heterogeneous area and, since bargaining is out of the question, either Jack or Jill is bound to experience a sense of resentment at the end of the day.

Titmuss gives no account of what happens when there is a fundamental conflict of values. Nor does he recognize the threat to individual liberties always implicit when philosopher-kings take the initiative and ultimately manipulate social values. There are, as it happens, all too often elements of a self-fulfilling prophecy concealed under a veneer of deference to the collective will: thus, for example, a sense of community may be the result rather than the cause of mixed neighbourhoods, and population movements into the new housing estates may in any case alter the electoral bias of the area in such a way as to ensure the voice-winning potential of similar policies in future. In social policy, the fact that a tiny spark can start a forest fire represents a genuine danger; and Titmuss most regrettably never really comes to grips with the dilemma that the views of the minority in a situation of conflict can all too easily become those of the group.

Fourth, Titmuss, although he had a sincere faith in the efficacy of centralized decision-making in the name of the social will, nonetheless gave no guidance as to the techniques politicians and bureaucrats are to employ in order to capture and measure consensus.

The problem is that concepts such as social needs and social relevance are imprecise, and that Titmuss does not say how they can in practice be accurately rather than impressionistically identified. Nor does he himself provide a theoretical framework for ranking states of dependency or comparing welfare projects at the margin in terms of quantifiable indices and hard calculus of utility. He offers no robust success-indicators that might be adopted by the welfare sector in place of the market sector's index of achievement, the rate of profit; gives little guidance on what criteria should be adopted in setting priorities as between services and in adjudicating disputes between them; and is somewhat too reticent to teach by example. Thus Titmuss' work is poor in case-histories of specific programmes illustrating how governments successfully determined the content of the collective consciousness and then reached the targets it prescribed. While this is a welcome antidote to the trivialities of the short-story approach to social policy, it leaves the reader confused as to the exact nature of the link between social intelligence and social welfare. Some cords are more umbilical than others; and there is in social policy, after all, an ever-present threat that the child will, by an act of deplorable perversity, give birth to the parent.

Titmuss does not say how information on the value consensus is to be collected or public opinion tapped. Indeed, he expressly rejects two important sources of intelligence, both of which have in common the useful property that they ask the consumer about his wants rather than informing him about his needs: the employment of the market mechanism in the welfare sector and of direct consumer participation in the planning of welfare services.

Titmuss' cavalier rejection of active democratic participation is a serious gap since it makes it difficult for administrators to consult directly with consumers. Such a lack of consultation is a source of inter-sector inequality: whereas a middle-class family can work together with their architect to plan the home of their dreams, the low-class family must accept the high-rise flat far from children's playgrounds, further still from the husband's place of work, that the welfare professionals deign to put at their disposal. Such a lack of consultation is likely, moreover, to leave the client with a sense of alienation rather than belonging: the dependent, like other people, want not just income-sharing but power-sharing as well, and are bound to feel resentment at the unequal distribution of the power cake. Gunnar Myrdal gives a sense of citizen involvement as one of the main reasons for general contentment in Sweden with the welfare state. He points out that 'when participation is on a low level, we should expect people to be more apt to feel that the regulations are imposed upon them from above and that they are being pushed around by "them" – the bosses, the bureaucrats and the oligarchies in the organisations, the strange and distant forces in Wall Street and Washington. This might breed feelings of resentment, and will anyhow frustrate people's feelings of solidarity and identification with the purposes of the regulations.'[10] Titmuss' model is remarkable for its lack of active community involvement (whether at the level of planning or at the level of execution of projects) and notable for its autocratic *étatisme*: the user is not consulted about his needs but is informed of them by politicians and bureaucrats acting, of course, on the basis of sound professional advice.

In practice, consumer choice in the welfare sector in often related to the role played by pressure groups; and it is therefore unfortunate that the lobby represents yet another notable absentee from Titmuss' system. In the absence of true participation, pressure groups typically represent claimants, social workers, detached academic observers and

other actors in the welfare drama; and yet such representation is
indirect (with the implicit threat that the organizations will not always
fully mirror the sentiments of their members), often undemocratic (as
where the groups are self-appointed spokesmen for citizens who do
not know of their existence, or where the leaders are not elected by the
rank and file), usually arbitrary (as in an attempt by administrators to
redeem an urban disaster area, where problems are multiple, criteria
complex, and it is not clear whom to consult), and always unequal
(since not all pressure-groups enjoy pressure-parity, making a dispute
between the representatives of the long-term mentally ill and the
representatives of the medical profession into a tragic farce). It is
unfortunate that Titmuss chose to neglect the role of pressure groups
in the decision-making process; for in the real world the emergence of
policies as an expression of values presupposes not only that people
are able to recognize their interests and formulate their convictions
(which need not coincide with some nebulous value consensus of
which they are blissfully unaware) but also that they are powerful and
militant enough to defend those interests and convictions through
pressure from below.

Titmuss believed that social policy is social action in accordance
with widely held social values; and had particular confidence in the
sensitivity of politicians and administrators to the wishes of the
majority. It is not impossible, however, that his confidence was
somewhat misplaced.

Consider first politicians. Because of the constraint of democracy
and the necessity to win an occasional yes/no vote at a general election
contested on a bundle of issues, such men may favour spectacular
projects which win them both prestige and support, and eschew both
the controversial and the boringly obscure. Similarly, they may offer
too many free gifts relative to what the community can afford in order
to gain votes, gambling on the ignorance of their masters. And they
may, if in touch with the value consensus of a nation whose business is
business, divert resources from the socialist philosopher in his ivory
tower to the sales executive in the semi-detached next door.

· It is likely in any case that Titmuss overestimated the accountability
of politicians to public opinion, and underestimated the extent to
which they see themselves, once elected into office, as an independent
estate in the land. If so, and recognizing that politicians are not
philosophers, there is a case for arguing that power should be disper-
sed rather than concentrated. Such dispersion could take the form of
political decentralization, since local government is at grass-roots level

often more sensitive to the needs of real people than are the patriarchs of Westminster. Such dispersion could, alternatively, take the form of the reprivatization of the welfare services, so as to enable, in the words of Milton Friedman, 'economic strength to be a check to political power rather than a reinforcement.'[11]

Titmuss recognized that political power can be a vital corrective to private economic power, an essential locus of countervailing power in a society hardly free of abuses. He failed to see, however, the extent to which political power can be a source of abuse in its own right, and neglected the danger that restrictions on individual freedom in one sphere can ultimately inhibit individual freedom in others. The threat of coercion is particularly prevalent in the field of welfare, since there political authority arrogates to itself not simply the right to regulate but the power to provide.

Titmuss, speaking of the government's wartime efforts to convince parents of the need to evacuate school children from the big urban agglomerations, comments as follows: 'The art of democratic persuasion, of making people feel confidence in the Government's plans, had to be practised.'[12] Here he seems content that plan should antedate persuasion, just as it does in the large corporation of the new industrial state. Yet if 'the art of democratic persuasion' is truly a powerful weapon, then it is not clear why politicians should ever first trouble to consult the elusive social matrix, the nebulous collective consciousness, rather than simply doing the deed and afterwards moulding attitudes in the image desired. Where such manipulation becomes a real threat, dispersion of power becomes a real alternative.

Consider now administrators. Titmuss stressed the dynamic nature of the welfare state and noted that our failure to recognize the 'all-pervasive character of social change' has in the past 'prevented us from understanding that all legislation is experimental and that a social service is a dynamic process – not a finished article.'[13] He called for flexibility and sensitivity in order to ensure that the social services change in accordance with changing social needs: 'The forces of the past in terms of how we live together in society create new situations; if the structure and functions of the social services cling too closely to the needs of the age when they originated, and if the interests which resist change become too powerful, these services will not meet the needs of the new situations. We shall not achieve a better balance between the needs of today and the resources of today by living out the destinies of tradition.'[14] It is, however, precisely the inertia generated from within the welfare Establishment itself which is in many cases responsible for retarded adaptation; and this Titmuss largely failed to grasp.

Titmuss neglected the extent to which groups within the state itself might have their own vested interests and particularistic objectives, and tended to assume a high degree of harmonious functional integration in the non-market sector. While he appreciated that extended professional division of labour and the resultant professional hierarchies based on fine classifications of expertise did generate professional inflexibilities, he nonetheless chose to ignore the implicit danger that commitment to the *status quo* will take precedence over the impassioned struggle for review and revision of policies. His choice is curious: it is naïve to assume that British welfare structures are markedly less the prisoners of interest than are American welfare industries when their cherished territory is threatened with invasion.

Titmuss recognized that managers of giant corporations in the private sector may have organizational goals of their own quite independent from those of their masters. He failed to see, however, that administrators of giant governmental departments and parastatal bodies may be similarly blinkered by interest and lured away from the pursuit of consensus by personal and private objectives such as job satisfaction (which may induce a service to do erudite research that society neither needs nor would want if it could understand the jargon of boffinism), security (which may prevent a service from winding itself up when it has served its purpose or decisively failed to do so), autonomy (which may cause a service to flee from the challenge of the interdepartmental committee into the cloistered isolation of parallel hierarchies) and growth (which may stimulate a service to expand, whatever rationalization it employs to itself and others, principally to generate more opportunities for promotion in a world of civil service imperialism). In order to attain its own organizational goals, a service may seek to impress with its successes and to avoid failures by concentrating scarce resources on the 'good risk' dependent who are most likely to make spectacular progress at minimum cost. Thus it may, for example, divert help from the stupid black to the bright black, or from the old lag to the bank clerk who once only put his hand in the till. Such a policy of playing safe is, needless to say, the opposite of what Titmuss intended when he called for selective discrimination.

The problem of organizational goals is compounded by the problem of organizational aggregation, and here we must note that Titmuss' belief in the efficacy of planning within the state sector is over-optimistic. The fact is that there is often an aimless proliferation of schemes for the simple reason that each group wants to be at the centre of one project or another; and the resultant bureaucratic tangle (combined with the inflexibilities of professionalism itself) need not represent a comprehensive and coordinated structure of services. In the real world, what passes for planning is often simply the compromise reached when one coalition of institutional interests exerts its countervailing power against another coalition of institutional interests in a house of power where each team tries to get the best possible deal for its own side. Power-rating may sway the balance in Whitehall, and strength does not mean wisdom: it only means that pensions men shout louder than hospitals men.

Devotion to organizational rather than wider social goals means that there may be inadequate opportunities for self-correcting mechanisms to originate within the social services themselves. It means that waste, delay, inefficiency and insensitivity may result from bureaucratic complexities and a general antipathy to change established patterns. It also means that a them-and-us situation may arise in the country; for the truth is that decision-makers in Westminster and Whitehall are not a representative cross-section of the population with a representative cross-section of social values.

No society is culturally homogeneous; each contains within itself a diversity of sub-cultures, of groups every one to a certain extent with its own ends, norms and perceptions. These sub-cultures, moreover, tend to be arranged not side by side in social space (in the pattern of separate but equal compartments analogous to the rings of an earthworm) but tend to take the form of an ascending scale of horizontal strata. Because of cultural segmentation and stratification (both variables of tertiary significance to Richard Titmuss), the balance of power within the machinery of state becomes of supreme importance; and here it must be admitted that leading decision-makers are likely to have middle-class backgrounds and outlooks on life. The democratic pluralist state may thus not be a parallelogram of forces such as to neutralize any particularistic outside interest precisely because, should all social groups not have the same values, those wielding public power are more likely to share the value system of other powerful élites (say, of businessmen in the market sector) than of the powerless and the dependent (say, of working-class black squatters in receipt of social security). The consequently selective filtering and screening of information, the consequently biased decisions that are made, may in turn leave the powerless and the dependent with a sense of alienation from their leaders; and may in truth engender apathy, frustration and resentment in place of that 'democratic identification with government'[15] which Titmuss so eagerly anticipated.

Part Two

SELECTIVITY

5 Selectivity

Titmuss believed that the state should provide a range of free welfare services. He also knew that resources are scarce and that there is a need to ration supply.[1] Clearly, even if resources are not to be rationed by price for all comers, there is at least a case for a dual system whereby those who can afford to pay for welfare rely on private provision, and the state (rather than providing welfare benefits indiscriminately) concentrates its help where the need is greatest and the ability to pay least. Titmuss, however, rejected such selectivity. Partly this was because of his belief, as we shall see later, that private enterprise in the field of welfare is a mixed blessing even for those who can pay; and partly it was because he was convinced that a dual system involves stigma.

Stigma means a loss of self-respect and personal dignity, a sense of guilt, of shame, of personal fault or failure. It means the sensation of second-class citizenship that revolts from discrimination. It means what Goffman calls 'spoiled identity',[2] since discrimination so easily becomes self-discrimination. To begin with this operates simply at the level of perception: 'If men and women come to think of (and feel) themselves as inferior persons, subordinated persons, then in part they stigmatise themselves, and in part they are reflecting what other people think or say about them.'[3] Later, however, the process of self-stigmatization seeps through to the level of action: 'If men are treated as a burden to others – if this is the role expected of them – then, in time, they will behave as a burden.'[4] Whether at the level of perception or at the level of action, such psychological damage is undesirable. It arises in a selective system in three ways:

First, there is the stage of trying to obtain private insurance or private treatment and failing because one is an actuarial bad risk. Naturally it would be uneconomic for the private market not to exclude those who cannot pay or are likely to make excessive demands on resources. It would also be unfair to the shareholders were private enterprise to redistribute the national income by, say, undertaking to provide 40-year mortgages to old-age pensioners. At the same time, however, this leaves the disadvantaged in a state of neglect. It may be that people ought to stand on their own feet and spend according to the dictates of their own conscience and purse; but they cannot be expected to buy services which the vendor is unprepared to sell.

The fact is that the private market does not provide adequate welfare services for such groups potentially at risk as the deprived child, the unmarried mother, the woman over 40 entering the labour force, the widow, the educationally deprived, the unemployed, the mentally handicapped and mentally ill, the physically handicapped (such as the deaf or the blind), the bedridden. It often neglects the coloured immigrant, the striker, the unsupported wife, the worker on a work-permit, the intermittently employed agricultural worker, or the 'elderly isolates and desolates'[5] of society. It does not provide treatment for the drug addict, the indigent, the impoverished schizophrenic newly discharged from hospital; and in America the whole urban ghetto is often declared an uninsurable risk. It must be remembered too that, in an increasingly mobile society, a number of those rejected by the private market will not have families to fall back on.[6]

It is possible that many of these potential losers apply for private insurance or treatment and are rejected without right of appeal. Not only is this a blatant denial of freedom of choice to large groups of would-be consumers, but lack of access to essential facilities leaves the felt and experienced need among such vulnerable groups of dependents without proper remedy; and it leaves them with the bitter taste of rejection, exclusion, powerlessness and lack of human dignity. In some way, whether on grounds of race, poverty, mental fitness or some other judgemental yardstick, society is seen to have expressed its disapproval and selected them out. Such stigmatization is the order of the day for many groups in modern society. It is, however, largely invisible: the insurance companies collect no statistics on 'the psychological and social harm they do to people'[7] in rejecting them or rating them as sub-standard, and it is hard to see in any case how a sense of stigma could be precisely quantified.

It has been argued that affluence and full employment will cause this first kind of stigma to disappear over time. The aim of state provision of social services, so the argument goes, should be self-liquidation as more and more people become eligible for privately-provided welfare: 'Such pockets of poverty and residual distress as still prevail will in time automatically and gracefully succumb to the determinism of growth. This will be achieved by a natural process of market levitation; all classes and groups will stand expectantly on the political right as the escalator of growth moves them up.'[8] The fallacy here is the assumption that the increase in command over resources will be evenly and proportionately distributed among spending units. Titmuss quotes American evidence for 1966 (one child in four and three elderly persons in ten living below the poverty line, a move towards greater inequalities in income and wealth) to support his contention that economic progress need not naturally lead to social progress without redistributive intervention by the state. The 'invisible resource allocation of the market'[9] in a dynamic economy will not solve the problem of poverty and thus of stigma associated with the rejection of application for private provision. *Embourgeoisement* is not the answer, the way out.

Second, there is the stigma associated with the means test that is administered to applicants for state welfare in order to guard the gate of state-provided cash benefits and free services against those who can afford to pay for private insurance, treatment and other welfare benefits. The aim being to reach the poor directly, they must first be separated out from a population which includes sheep as well as goats, non-poor as well as poor.

The means-test is a deterrent to abuse and aims to help the poor by sparing them the need to share scarce welfare resources with all and sundry. Unfortunately however, welfare provided on a discriminatory, means-tested basis has a tendency to 'foster both the sense of personal failure and the stigma of a public burden'. Clearly, 'the fundamental objective of all such tests of eligibility is to keep people out; not to let them in. They must, therefore, be treated as applicants or supplicants; not beneficiaries or consumers.'[10] Yet 'it is a regrettable but human fact that money (and the lack of it) is linked to personal and family self-respect.'[11] No poor person wants to stand up and define or identify himself as poor, for to do so would hence be 'to declare, in effect, "I am an unequal person".'[12] Such a punitive process of selection, because it means a 'humiliating loss of status, dignity or self-respect',[13] is an insult to humanity.

Quite apart from the indignities involved, moreover, means-testing is undesirable because of the administrative problem. Any test that acknowledges the fundamental truth that 'there are no standard families with standard or uniform requirements'[14] becomes an administrative nightmare, Titmuss argued, due to the multiplicity of variables that must be taken into account. And these variables do not remain constant. Circumstances are in a continual state of flux caused by births, adoption, children leaving school, marriage and remarriage, desertion, separation, divorce, illness, disablement, retirement, death, fires and disasters, unemployment, a new job (possibly with a pay increase only just keeping pace with inflation), a new house (with a different rent), boarders, inheritance, institutional care for aged parents, capital appreciation, windfalls and numerous other factors influencing the resources and responsibilities of spending units. Hence, even if meaningful means-testing of families could be carried out, the results are likely very quickly to become out of date.

Means-testing also makes it difficult to deal with urgent needs. In the case of, say, an evicted family with an unemployed father where an individual experiences a spell of sickness, the emergency must be dealt with immediately, and without the delay imposed by complex administrative formalities. In any case, these formalities are bound heavily to penalize the most ignorant (who may well be the most needy). There are a multitude of *different* means tests (at least 1,500 are administered by local authorities in England and Wales in the health, education, child care, housing and other welfare fields) and in the past we have 'overestimated the potentialities of the poor, without help, to understand and manipulate an increasingly complex *ad hoc* society.'[15] Such people are not only stigmatized by welfare but may be excluded from it (not least where they have multiple needs involving multiple tests): 'Who helps them, I wonder, to fill up all those forms?'[16]

A negative income tax system operated through the Pay As You Earn network would help remove this administrative burden from the dependent by making benefits (albeit in the form of money, not services) automatically available, and based on a computerized code number. It would, however, face the same insuperable difficulties as any other test in attempting to estimate resources and needs, to keep track of changes over time, or to deal with urgent needs. It simply does not make sense to deal with this year's emergency by applying a code-number derived from last year's data, based on a P.60 which may be hopelessly out of date.[17] Naturally, employers could be asked to provide the Inland Revenue not with annual data but with weekly or monthly data, so as to keep the tax-code up to date in a non-static world; and this data could then be married on a continuous basis with other relevant data (as where, for example, husband and wife are assessed separately for income tax). All of this, however, is a waste of administrative resources (including the resources of private employers) and might not even be feasible (due to the multitude and complexity of ever-changing variables). As Titmuss says: 'What I find frightening is the extraordinary administrative naïvety of those who argue in such terms for "selectivity".'[18]

Not only is any means test bound to be administratively unwieldy, but it is not able to deal mechanistically with the mass of difficult value judgements that must be made at all stages in defining criteria for eligibility. The basic decision is, of course, to specify in what precise financial circumstances an individual qualifies for free state care; but this in turn raises other important questions and ultimately involves complicated social values. For example: Should men who do not work be better off than men who do (the wage-stop)? Should a distinction be made between earned and unearned incomes? Should the test be a wealth test or 'should income tests and charges disregard capital assets, house property, discretionary trusts, education covenants, insurance policies, reversionary interests, fringe benefits, tax-free lump sums, share options, occupational benefits in kind and suchlike?'[19] Should wives be encouraged to go out to work? Should one distinguish qualitatively as to the cause of dependency (the same zero income, for example, might be earned by a striker, a layabout, a disabled war hero, or a student in the process of acquiring socially useful skills)? Naturally, once considerations of ethics and equity are brought in, 'computers cannot answer these questions.'[20] There is no escape from the human decision-maker.

Third, there is the stigma attached to separate provision, partly because the special facilities provided are clearly ear-marked for failures and inadequates, and partly because residual provision is invariably inferior provision. The truth is that 'separate discriminatory services for poor people have always tended to be poor quality services,'[21] second-class services aimed at second-class consumers excluded from the middle-class world of welfare and conscious of that exclusion.

The inferiority of public compared with privately provided services is to some extent a question of finance: 'Insofar as they are able to recruit at all for education, medical care and other services, they tend to recruit the worst rather than the best teachers, doctors, nurses, administrators and other categories of staff upon whom the quality of service so much depends.'[22] As far as the poor are concerned, however, 'if the quality of personal service is low, there will be less freedom of choice and more felt discrimination.'[23] Such felt discrimination is not an unintended outcome but part of the system. Its roots may be found historically in a past society which attempted to reconcile compassion with individualism by treating the poor as the indigent, a public burden for whom a safety net had to be provided, but subject to the expression of disapproval.

Rationing by shame and inferior quality of services provided is, however, no longer acceptable as a deterrent in the way that it was acceptable at the time of the New Poor Law of 1834. Then, 'shame was needed to make the system work.'[24] Nowadays, the collectivity is more likely to feel that the dependent should not be sanctioned with stigma, and that those who provide welfare should not see it as their duty to punish the recipient for some supposed dereliction or failing on his part.

To avoid the cumulative and demoralizing effects of rejection on the individual, therefore, Professor Titmuss believed that social welfare services should be provided free of charge and as of right to all citizens, and depend on their needs but not on their means. In place of a selectivist system, where the state withers away until it performs merely a residual function, Titmuss believed that a universalist structure of services must be made available to all, since liberation from state intervention is bound to increase the incidence of experienced disapprobation in society. The great majority of people using the National Health Service do not feel stigmatized, and the reason is that the Service is known and felt to be universalist in scope.[25] The same infrastructure of facilities is used by the non-poor and the poor alike (i.e. by those who *could* pay for private attention as well as those who could not). Selection is avoided and the dependent (say, the out-of-work or the aged) keep their self-respect. In Britain, just as a cat can look at a king, so a West Indian labourer can share a ward with a Professor of Social Administration.

The avoidance of stigma is secured by opening social welfare services to all regardless of class, colour or income. Naturally this great benefit substantially raises the cost of provision. But against that cost must be set the fact that universalism not only negates a previous negation but also constitutes a definite affirmation by making a constructive contribution to social growth in three important ways. These are the covering of social costs by social provision, the furtherance of a heightened sense of social integration, and the creation of a framework within which to plan the redistribution of life-chances. We will examine these social benefits in Part Three.

But what about selective utilisation ie. more middle class use of NHS?

6 Part Two: an Evaluation

Titmuss warns against 'outer rather than inner observation.'[1] Yet he himself was guilty of this very fault. His theories tend to neglect the subjective dimension of how people (especially dependent people) actually and in fact feel in particular situations, and tend instead to focus on how the philosopher presumes they ought to feel. Nowhere is this neglect of the subjective dimension more apparent than in the case of stigma.

Titmuss expresses his own perceptions of stigma (which are absolutely central to his whole system of thought) and does so with considerable force and conviction. What really matters, however, is the self-perceptions that dependent people themselves enjoy; and here it must be confessed that the ordinary citizen probably does not always think as the middle-class academic expects him to do.

Titmuss' view of the world loses much of its persuasive power once we recognize that means-testing is not the unique source of stigma, and may not even be an important source of spoiled identity to the poor. The welfare services, after all, even if they truly are services strictly non-judgemental in nature, do not exist in an ethical vacuum: a girl, for example, who in a puritanical society has an illegitimate child will be so stigmatized by the outside world that she will hardly notice the shabby décor and tasteless lunch of the charity hospital where she goes for care because she is unable to afford private attention. This is not to say that the décor ought to be shabby or the lunch tasteless, only that she will probably think that it is society and not welfare which has tested her and found her deficient.

Social values are a hard taskmaster, and are themselves a much greater threat to personal dignity (a much greater cause of spoiled identity) than the need to submit to any means test. Moreover, the greatest source of stigma is likely, in a competitive society, to derive from the continuous process of selection and rejection that the individual experiences in the market sector from the day he leaves school until the day he goes into hospital with stomach pains brought on by failure to win promotion in a status-oriented and status-conscious world. A man who is denied private insurance is not likely to be in a prestigious and secure occupation, and has probably been treated to rejection rather than selection from a very early age. He is no doubt low-paid, which in an acquisitive society where men are judged by earning and spending means stigma in its own right: he conspicuously has less command over the goods and services society identifies with 'the good life'. And he will return to the world of the low-paid, low-status stigmatized once his ulcers (caused by repeated rejection in the market sector) have been cured (by universalist treatment in the welfare sector). It is not clear whether such a man would really experience a sense of stigma if he were means-tested prior to treatment; and Titmuss was wrong not to probe more deeply into the actual attitudes that arise in both sectors, or into the way in which they dovetail.

Moreover, as Professor Pinker has pointed out (thereby antagonizing Titmuss[2]), the state services themselves may actually have a tendency to stigmatize. Pinker argues in effect that it is debatable (and worthy of debate) whether one society can have two contradictory central value systems, and points out that people socialized in a market economy characterized by a cash nexus may in reality experience stigma by the very process of receiving unilateral gifts provided free of charge by the state. He puts the problem as follows: 'As we grow up, the most authentic rights we acquire and exercise are those we use in the roles of buyers and sellers in the market-place. We do not have to be persuaded that we have rights to what we buy. The idea of paying through taxes or holding authentic claims by virtue of citizenship remains largely an intellectual conceit of the social scientist and the socialist. For the majority the idea of participant citizenship in distributive processes outside the market-place has very little meaning. Consequently most applicants for social services remain paupers at heart.'[3]

The idea is that dependency rather than equivalency is for most people psychologically unpleasant at the best of times, and is bound by its very nature to be humiliating in what is chiefly not a citizenship-oriented but a money-oriented society. People tend to feel stigmatized by handouts in a system which they regard as one of sanctions (even where the handouts are avowedly only compensation for social costs borne by the few on behalf of the many); and tend to be unaware of their inalienable rights to welfare or of how they acquired them. What people do know is that the less prestigious social groups appear to require more care, with the result that care itself comes to acquire stigma by association. There is clearly a case here for education for citizenship, to inform people of their rights, to persuade them that all social groups benefit from social services and, most of all, to preach the gospel of community and fellowship. Titmuss acknowledged the first two functions of education for citizenship but would have rejected the third: perceptions of community and fellowship are, after all, expected to arise spontaneously and without the need for propaganda. It could nonetheless be maintained that until the idea of a national family has firmly taken root, consuming without paying will remain in itself a self-stigmatizing action, and that a hint of propaganda in the here-and-now would have filled a definite gap in the model.

Curiously, Titmuss seems to have recognized, at least in the case of income maintenance, that people often experience guilt at getting something for nothing: writing about superannuation, he insisted that 'people do not want to be *given* rights to pensions, but ..... want to *earn* them by their contributions.'[4] If, however, this is a good description of people's psychology, then there is surely a case for user-charges for all services so that customers can convince themselves they are buying a right. Titmuss unfortunately did not follow up this line of argument and tended as a general rule to ignore the possibility that unilateral gifts may themselves come to represent stigma. As result, he understandably also neglected the likelihood that such stigmatization will vary as between social classes. Yet such variation is a not uncommon feature of the modern British welfare state.

Thus the specialist seen on the National Health Service may to some have stigmatizing properties. Partly this is due to the fact that he is not paid directly: whereas in the private sector the customer clearly establishes a *right* to a service by virtue of the *payment* that he makes, in the state sector the customer takes without giving and may in consequence experience a sense of personal failure. Partly too this is due to social stratification: the specialist may appear to stigmatize not just by his superior expertise but by his superior class background, as demonstrated by his manner and his accent. Understandably, the well-to-do might escape stigma arising on either account. They pay taxes, often at higher rates, and can convince themselves that the *quid* more than covers the *quo*; and they often share a common class background with the doctor (which leads to a sense of one professional talking to another). There is clearly a need to disaggregate in order to isolate the subjective perception known as stigma. This, however, Titmuss does not do, since he associates stigma primarily with denial of access and with entry barriers to a service.

Furthermore, the least glamorous and least prestigious services are likely to have the most stigmatizing properties: thus a man might not feel at all debased in accepting a means-tested university scholarship who would be mortified to accept Supplementary Benefits, although both services might represent an equal drain on national resources. And, as it happens, the well-to-do are more likely to apply for the grant, the poor more likely to apply for national assistance.

The case for positive discrimination rests to a large extent on Titmuss' theories of stigma. Positive discrimination implies direction of resources without stigma towards a particular group. Here, of course, the question is not (as it is with a means test) whom to exclude but whom to include more intensively. Whether or not this can be done without stigma is another matter. Some groups may feel stigmatized by being selected (and therefore branded as deficient); and there is no *a priori* reason to think that the people in Plowden's Educational Priority Areas do not experience a collective sense of shame. There may also be a conflict between economic necessity and welfare objectives where teachers and doctors in deprived areas get extra 'dirty jobs' money compared with those who work with the rich and articulate: such differentials may be functionally necessary to attract social welfare professionals into understaffed areas (and retain them there), and yet still induce a sense of stigma in the body of consumers should they learn the percentage value of their inferiority. Again, just as some groups may feel stigmatized by being selected, so others may feel stigmatized by being rejected (and therefore dismissed as less worthy). If a university discriminates in favour of blacks and browns, it is by definition discriminating against yellows and whites; and those latter persons whose education is impeded on grounds of colour or social background may well feel stigmatized by the denial of equal treatment. It is in any case by no means obvious how a society ought to discriminate in favour of the poor without the use of a means test. Naturally, such discrimination can be geographical (where the deprived are concentrated in ghettoes, slums and urban disaster areas); but geographical discrimination only picks up a minority of the poor where they are scattered throughout the entire population (the case of old-age pensioners, who moreover benefit little from the construction of new schools in Educational Priority Areas); and discrimination on the basis of other broad categories is prone to perversity. Without the use of a means test, it is impossible to tell a poor white from a rich black, and a mistake as to which man most needs help not only frustrates the objectives of social policy but engenders a sense of rejection in the citizen left behind.

Finally, in concluding our discussion of stigma it is important to note that some areas of the welfare state cannot by their nature be universal in scope. Selection mechanisms must, because of the constraint of scarce resources, be applied, and some candidates are bound to be selected out. This is the situation with higher education, where the rise of the meritocracy is in consequence often associated with a widespread sense of failure on the part of those who failed to make the grade and stay the course. This is also the situation with hopeless cases, where a welfare professional declines to succour an applicant who nonetheless (perhaps unjustly) expects treatment. Even an aging down-and-out with chronic kidney trouble can still feel a sense of resentment when he learns that his turn on the machine will not come until his case is 'off the books'.

Part Three

UNIVERSALISM

7 Universalism 1: Social Costs and Social Benefits

Economic growth is not a problem in economics alone; and Titmuss therefore regarded it as deplorable that excessive compartmentalization has caused us to neglect the interaction between economic and social policy. Such neglect is a serious matter since there is in fact a 'fundamental conflict between welfare and economic growth, between economic and social growth'.[1] A collectivity that wants rising standards of living must hence be prepared, first, to compensate those of its members who suffer from the social disservices, diswelfares, disutilities and insecurities that result from progress; and, second, to erect that valuable social infrastructure of essential services which is complementary to growth in the private sector but not provided by it. In this chapter we shall examine these two reasons for the provision of social benefits to cover social costs.

Consider first the need to compensate citizens for social diswelfares suffered on behalf of the collectivity, as in the case of enforced unemployment or compulsory mobility (occupational and geographical) in a fluid economy. Technological and scientific advance brings, it is generally conceded, great benefits to the group; but it may also mean that some men are rendered redundant by automation and driven into early retirement because they have the misfortune to possess (through no fault of their own) obsolete skills in a world of extensive division of labour, labour-specificity and often of long retraining periods. Such redundancies (such man-made social costs) are not likely to be randomly distributed, but are likely to be analogous to a regressive tax which is a greater burden on poorer than on richer households and hence promotes social inequalities: after all, the groups most vulnerable to unemployment are likely to be the poor, the unskilled, the underprivileged, who can least afford to pay the costs of social change.

Other kinds of social diswelfare may be more diffuse. This is the case with the problem of unmerited handicap (the handicap of, say, deprived children of unmarried mothers; or the objects of ethnic and religious prejudice; or the 'victims of the mistakes we make in our educational systems by wrongly stigmatizing and rejecting people as "failures" '[2]). This is the case too with the problem of the aged now that urbanization and the breakdown of kinship ties have led to changes in family life such that children no longer accept the responsibility for their parents. Lengthening of life-expectancy at the same time as the institution of smaller families means that parents would in any case have fewer grown-up children to rely on in the dependency created by old age.

Nor should we ignore the subjective aspects of social costs. The worker disabled for life in a factory accident or by an industrial disease will suffer from loss of status as well as loss of earnings, not least if his wife goes out to work to make ends meet. The man of fifty who is made redundant and is unable to obtain another job will suffer from reduced earning and spending power and from spoiled life-chances, but also from a sense of failure generated in the market sector: 'Have we really any conception of the psychological effects on people of a continual process of social rejection and exclusion? Yet economic growth tends continuously to build ever higher these gateways to life and freedom of choice, and to widen the area over which credentialism rules; the crowd outside finds it harder to clamber over, squeeze through, or look over the top.[3] Loss of status can be 'a serious injury to the personality',[4] and yet such stigmatization is an increasing threat (at least for the labourer) in the modern economy: 'The dominating characteristics of industrial conditions in the West during the past few decades have been, from the point of view of the worker, irregularity and impermanence. Unemployment, short-time working, the decay of skills as a result of technological change, and the rationalization of production have all spelled, in the worker's psychology, irregularity and uncertainty.'[5] In the modern economy, there is greater opportunity not only for individual failure but for consciousness of individual failure. The incidence of both the fact and the perception is likely to be greater among the low-paid than among the meritocracy; and yet both social groups are expected to give the same sense of security and hope to their children.

The reference to children reminds us that the secondary effects of social change may be delayed, and that material and psychological casualties may not become noticeable for several generations.

Consider the case of a society about to industrialize: 'If those who are first subjected to industrial change have had stable childhoods within a coherent, meaningful social order, then they may be able psychologically to withstand the pressure of change. Their children and grandchildren may be more likely to show the psychological effects of the long-drawn-out processes of industrialization. They will have been reared in an unstable culture by parents without a sure sense of direction or purpose.'[6] Similarly, such instability may result from bad housing conditions and poverty in an environment characterized by the social neglect which results from generations of laissez-faire liberalism. Here it is the group rather than the individual who is to blame: 'The devil in this particular piece seems to have more of the character of Bentham than of Freud.'[7]

In discussions of social time, the period in question can be very long, as the example of the Second World War shows. The poor health and neglected state of many of the young evacuees of 1939 was due not simply to unemployment and poverty in the inter-war years but to the First World War as well, for it was then that the parents were young. In the years from 1914 to 1918, many children were employed for thirty or even forty hours per week in addition to their schooling, and others left school altogether to take jobs. Then, on top of this exhaustion and ignorance, there was a lack of medical attention as more and more doctors and nurses got involved in the war-effort. Finally, the absence, disablement or death of the father in the War harmed the emotional growth of the young.

Similar points must be borne in mind when we calculate the delayed effects of the Second World War. There is, for example, the case of 'children who, because of the closing down of clinics in some areas or their absence in others, were left at the end of the war with uncorrected squints'; and of 'children stigmatised – perhaps for life – as hereditarily "backward" because of the disorganisation of their schooling during the war'; and also of 'mothers left with pelvic damage after childbirth as a result of the effects of the war on the maternity services'.[8] When we reflect that many of the children stigmatized by the Second World War were the children of parents stigmatized by the First, it becomes clear that social costs may be cumulative and also that the relevant time-span or accounting-period can be lengthy: tomorrow's dependencies may easily be the result of yesterday's changes in life-chances. Nor can society ever expect the final reckoning to be presented in terms of a set of precise estimates: 'The biological cost of any war, let alone war on civilian society, can never be summed up with any finality. There are the men and women who are maimed and prevented from marrying, the children who have died because of a worsening in their physical environment, the adolescents who have contracted tuberculosis for some reason arising from the war, the babies who have not been born and cannot now be born, and all the defects and injuries, subtle and gross, which one generation hands on in irrevocable fashion to succeeding ones.'[9]

Society must recognize that the costs of change whether material or psychological, whether currently generated or the heritage from the past, cannot be allowed to 'lie where they fall'. Social action is inescapable to compensate the victims of change once it is understood that the casualties are not simply the fault of individual action but are at least in part the necessary diswelfares that the individual suffers in order that the group as a whole might thrive. Often those whose own life-chances are damaged are 'the social pathologies of other people's progress'[10]; and society as a group must collectively choose, once it has become aware of the 'social theory of causality'[11] (analogous to the germ theory of disease) to relieve those struck down by the 'modern choleras of change'.[12] The point is that social causes indicate a need for social treatment, and that the laissez-faire solution of allowing social costs to lie where they fall is not only inhuman but inconsistent: since it is society which receives the benefits, it is society which ought to pay the bill.

Because a substantial part of social welfare provided by the state 'represents some element of compensation for disservice caused by society'[13], the redistribution associated with such welfare need not represent 'betterment of condition' or 'net lessening of inequality'. It might simply mean the restoration of the status quo ante: 'The emphasis today on "welfare" and the "benefits of welfare" often tends to obscure the fundamental fact that for many consumers the services are not essentially benefits or increments to welfare at all; they represent partial compensation for disservices, for social costs and social insecurities which are the product of a rapidly changing industrial-urban society. They are part of the price we pay to some people for bearing part of the cost of other people's progress.'[14] Such a price is not redistributive but anti-redistributive; the state simply redresses a previous grievance.

Since much of welfare is outright compensation, it is important for it to be both non-stigmatizing and non-judgemental.

As regards stigma, it would clearly be grossly unjust to insult the victim of social change by means-testing him to see if he can afford to bear the cost of other people's progress; and thus, even if stigma were not evil in its own right, any satisfactory means test would have to distinguish *cause of need* as well as *ability to pay* once a state of dependency had been identified. Understandably, because science is not up to disaggregating the complex causes of a given dependency (causes which may to a considerable extent be shrouded in the mists of time), there is a strong presumption that no means test can ever be truly just.

Again, there should be no judgemental basis for provision of welfare to those in need. It is vital to be tolerant and not to express an anti-sociological value judgement by branding some people as 'problems': 'Labels may be fashionable in a century of science, but when they attach and imply hypothetical inferiorities – of race, religion, "intelligence" or behaviour – they are fundamentally undemocratic and – in the present writer's view – harmful.'[15] A mere reference to social deviation implies, by virtue of the very words we use, an undesirable value judgement: 'Language is not a mere symbolic tool of communication. By describing someone as deviant we express an attitude; we morally brand him and stigmatise him with our value judgement.'[16] Such a judgement is unscientific and incorrect, since the deviant might not be deviant in their essence but merely deviant because of the social situation in which they find themselves.

Titmuss states categorically that 'social deviation, like crime, is a social ill or a "social problem"',[17] a social fact to be explained by other social facts. Here we see the justification and role for truly *social* policy. In the case of poverty, for example, the causes may be collective rather than individual, and it is therefore regrettable that we have so often in the past 'sought too diligently to find the causes of poverty among the poor and not in ourselves'.[18] In the past, our frame of reference has been too narrow and 'poverty engineering has thus been abstracted from society.'[19] In the future, we should adopt a more sociological approach to social policy, and attempt to grasp that the diseconomies associated with economic growth may well engender social rights to compensation.

It would, of course, be wrong to think that such compensation can be precisely assessed, particularly since the costs of progress may be psychological as well as material. Here as elsewhere in the social sciences, accurate calculations are an abstraction. Here as elsewhere too, however, the quantitative tends to push out the qualitative until we find ourselves 'saddled with a new form of Gresham's Law: monetary information – or dollar number magic – of *lesser* signific-

ance tends to displace other information which may be of *greater*
significance.'[20] This tendency is dangerous, for the fact that damages
cannot be exactly assessed does not mean that society should neglect
to compensate its victims.

The problems of social costs will become more acute in the future
due to the acceleration of economic, social, scientific and technological
change, and it is thus tragic that economists ignore these costs in
making their calculations:

> The social costs of change rarely enter into the calculations and
> models of economists. They measure what they can more easily
> count. As yet, we cannot quantify in material terms social misery
> and ill-health, the effects of unemployment, slum life and Negro
> removal, the denial of education and civil rights, and the cumulative
> side effects from generation to generation of allowing cynicism and
> apathy to foster and grow. These are some of the costs which
> appear inescapably to accompany social and technical change. They
> are not embodied in any index of 'real' income *per capita*. We have,
> therefore, to remind ourselves continuously about their reality,
> partly because we happen to be living in a scientific age which tends
> to associate the measureable with the significant; to dismiss as
> intangible that which eludes measurement; and to reach conclusions
> on the basis of only those things which lend themselves to measure-
> ment. Mathematical casework is not yet, I am glad to say, on the
> horizon.[21]

Consider now the second reason for the provision of social benefits
to cover social costs, namely the need to supply essential services
complementary to growth in the private sector but not provided by it.
To some extent this follows on logically from the need to compensate
the victims of change: after all, in a number of cases society has been
forced into paying the costs of change by the fact that alternative
compensation has simply not been forthcoming. One of the principal
reasons for the state's acceptance of the obligation to compensate (in
cash or in kind) for loss of income or other injury to life-chances is the
fact that 'scientifically, statistically and legally, it is becoming increasingly difficult in all modern societies – capitalist, socialist or mixed –
to identify the causal agents of diswelfare and charge them with the
costs.'[22] Social costs cannot be shifted back to the causal agent where
the culprit cannot be found, and hence the costs are transferred to the
state (which is already in any case coping with those social disutilities

which have unambiguously social causes): 'Non-discriminating universalist services are in part the consequence of unidentifiable causality.'[23] The alternative to social provision is to allow the costs to lie where they fall.

Redress of grievances through the courts is expensive, complicated and inadequate; and this is to be expected in an increasingly complex society where it is easy to identify neither tort-feasors nor victims of change. The difficulty increases with the passage of social time (where pathologies accelerate and become cumulative so that today's dependency may date back to a cause two centuries ago). Nowadays causality of disservice is often multiple and so diffuse as to 'defy the wit of law'[24]. In such a case there is no alternative to state welfare provisions since private fault cannot be established: 'Can we, in providing benefits, distinguish between "faults" in the individual (moral, psychological or social), the legal concept of "fault" in private accident insurance, and the "faults" of change? Put concretely, can we say when a coal miner living in a slum house contracts tuberculosis and needs medical care plus income maintenance for himself and his family, that the mine owner in the past or the National Coal Board today is responsible, or the landlord of the house, or the man himself or the whole community?'[25]

The inability to assign 'fault' reminds us that 'fault' itself might be social. Where this is the case, a diswelfare resulting apparently from individual causes might in fact have social causes. Take the case of road accidents: 'During this century more people have been injured by the automobile in the USA than in all the wars that country has been engaged in – the First World War, the Second World War, the Korean War and the Vietnam War.'[26] Looked at from one perspective, the car industry seems to impose a heavy cost on the community: 'In Britain in 1965 there were nearly 400,000 road casualties, one-quarter of them classified as "serious" and demanding prolonged hospital care.'[27] Looked at from another perspective, however, the motor-car may be thought of as part of a way of life, so that it is that amorphous way of life which is 'at fault'. The existence of road accidents does not necessarily make the car industry guilty, or mean that it ought to contribute towards hospitals and insurance benefits (despite the fact that at present in Britain about half of road accident victims must rely on state compensation in the absence of any tort damages at all).[28] Again, to take another example, there is the case of the firm that goes bankrupt because it produces out-of-date commodities in a changing society. Such a firm should not have to pay unemployment compensation or finance retraining of workers with obsolescent skills any more than the injured party should have to go without. Here there is simply no 'guilty' party needing to make amends for economic and social change. It is worthwhile remembering too that a bankrupt firm, even where as guilty as sin, does not typically have the means to pay damages. Both of these cases illustrate how the two reasons for state provision of social benefits to cover social costs may converge: not only does the problem in each case have a social cause (implying the need for social compensation), but adequate private redress is forthcoming in neither (indicating the complementarity between state provision and private activity).

Many are unaware that social growth, rather than inhibiting economic growth, is actually complementary to it. Yet the truth is that there is no necessary contradiction between compassion and efficiency, since welfare can make a 'positive contribution to productivity as well as reinforcing the social ethic of human equality'.[29] The social services are thus an important part of the life of the community: 'The social services (however we define them) can no longer be considered as "things apart"; as phenomena of marginal interest, like looking out of the window on a train journey. They are part of the journey itself. They are an integral part of industrialization'.[30]

Professor Titmuss had occasion to draw the attention of the Government of Mauritius to the significant handmaiden role that could be played in the process of economic development by a national health service:

> Both the incidence and duration of periods of incapability for work can be reduced. If there were better preventive services, there would be less illness. If there were better curative services, there would be a swifter return to work. If there were better rehabilitation services, there would be less economic waste and less drain on the medical and public assistance budgets. If the maternity and child welfare services were improved, the women of Mauritius could bear healthier children with fewer debilitating pregnancies and employers would benefit from a new generation of workers with a greater output and more regular attendance at work.[31]

The national health service is clearly a valuable external economy to employers, as is borne out by British experience: 'It is estimated that in industrial areas in Britain today up to one-third of all hospital out-patient attendances are attributable to factory accidents.... These are social costs of production which have been transferred – so far as medical care is concerned – to a "social service"'.[32] In many such cases, the tort-feasors are known. For example: 'Men employed in the chemical industry are about thirty times more likely than the general population to die of cancer of the bladder.'[33] Yet Titmuss does not call for the guilty to provide better compensation, and points instead to the present state of neglect: 'For an individual worker the connection between the medical diagnosis of cancer and the nature of his employment and contact with the causal agent may never be made or made too late. The worker, his widow and children will thus have been denied industrial disease benefits and legal compensation.'[34]

Consider too the example of motorways, parking spaces, town planning, slum clearance, meters, traffic police, driving tests, hospitals and insurance benefits in the state sector (because of accidents and air pollution from fumes). These products and services are complementary to the motor car, but are provided free of charge by the community. The reason is that willy nilly only society is in a position to deal in these benefits: 'How should these positive, correcting, preventive, and compensatory services be paid for, and who should be responsible for providing them? They cannot be bought and paid for in the private market by the individual motorist. They cannot be insured against in the private market. There is no monetary profit in the provision of anti-air pollution services, for instance.'[35] In the absence of state action, in a situation where private costs seriously diverge from social costs, the result is all too likely to be no action at all.

8 Universalism II: Integration and Involvement

Professor Titmuss believed that 'it is now (or should be) an objective of social policy to build the identity of a person around some community with which he is associated.'[1] This integrative objective 'is an essential characteristic distinguishing social policy from economic policy'.[2] The market mechanism is too individualist to conceive of the organic and neglects the vital importance (both positive and normative) of harmonious community relations and a sense of involvement. It is clearly not suitable for a subject such as social administration whose 'primary areas of unifying interest are centred in those social institutions that foster integration and discourage alienation'.[3]

Titmuss warned the Government of Tanganyika that the decline of traditional local communities might lead to a moral vacuum, a state of Durkheimean 'anomie' characterized by excessive individuation and an absence of satisfactory relationships: 'Towns and villages which have been long established have, like the houses of which they consist, often developed characteristics which favour the maintenance of a satisfactory community structure within them. This is, however, seldom the case in rapidly growing villages and towns, many of which have in other countries suffered not only the ravages of communicable disease, but the breakdown of community life and the substitution of an amorphous group of which the members admit responsibility to no one, with consequent deterioration of ethical and legal standards and the spread of mental distress.'[4]

This tragic picture of aloneness must be contrasted with the healthy spectacle of togetherness presented by the example of Britain at war. Then opportunities arose to play an active part in the community and brought people closer together, overcoming moral isolation and preventing any mass breakdown of mental health despite long periods of almost daily bombardment and the threat of invasion:

The civilian war of 1939–45, with its many opportunities for service in civil defence and other schemes, also helped to satisfy an often inarticulate need; the need to be a wanted member of society. Circumstances were thus favourable to fuller self-expression, for there was plenty of scope for relieving a sense of inferiority and failure.... It could conceivably be argued that to some people the air raids brought security – not the security which spells passive acquiescence, but that which allows and encourages spontaneity. The onset of air raids followed a long period of unemployment. One thing that unemployment had not stimulated was an active body or mind. It might be suggested – though it cannot yet be asserted – that the absence of an increase in neurotic illness among the civilian population during the war was connected with the fact that to many people the war brought useful work and an opportunity to play an active part within the community.... New aims for which to live, work that satisfied a larger number of needs, a more cohesive society, fewer lonely people; all these elements helped to offset the circumstances which often lead to neurotic illness.[5]

The 'social and psychological sense of community' is a broad concept, but one which may be equated with 'the concept and consciousness of "who is my neighbour?"'[6] It is a desirable sensation, for man, a sociable as well as a social animal, is happiest when most integrated in the group. Social policy ought therefore to be seen as being concerned not simply with the relief of individual needs but with the furtherance of a sensation of common citizenship (which necessitates common facilities and equality of access as of right and without the socially divisive stigma of a means test).

Equality of access to the universalist social services contributes to social integration and combats the sensation or reality of social discrimination. Furtherance of unity ought to be a major objective of a national health service, as Titmuss and his colleagues told the Government of Tanganyika: 'We want to see a health service developing which will not be separate and aloof from the life of the nation but an expression and reinforcement of national unity.'[7] So should avoidance of discrimination: 'It is now widely accepted that in all sectors of the economy there is a national need to diminish both the absolute fact and the psychological sense of social and economic discrimination.'[8] Four examples concerning the National Health Service will help to make clear the socially integrative role of the welfare state:

First, like the state educational services, the National Health Service has 'a community relations or non-discriminatory integrative function'[9] insofar as it helps to integrate racial minorities and thus to combat that ethnic conflict which might result from denial of participation or felt exclusion.

In the United States, poor blacks excluded from the profit-motivated private medical services and forced into a sub-standard state system feel stigmatized and rejected on grounds of colour. This dual welfare system, rather than furthering a sense of 'one society'[10], actually increases those tensions that arise out of powerlessness, alienation and frustration. The example of the United States shows that 'more prosperity and more violence may be one of the contradictions in a system of unfettered private enterprise and financial power oblivious to moral values and social objectives.'[11]

In Britain, on the other hand, pink and non-pink people share adjacent beds in hospital. In America, voluntary hospitals 'have public wards for indigents which tend to be full of black people. This can be contrasted with the integrated wards and outpatient departments of British hospitals under the National Health Service.'[12] Ethnic integration is fostered by the absence of formal barriers to access other than need in a system of medical care available to all on a universalistic basis; and the National Health Service thus plays its part in combating a major social ill, racial discrimination, to which the market mechanism would have turned a blind eye. Clearly, 'civil rights legislation in Britain to police the commercial insurance companies . . . . . would be a poor and ineffective substitute for the National Health Service.'[13]

Second, the National Health Service provides the same treatment to manual and non-manual workers, as indeed to the retired and the unemployed. With the introduction of the National Health Service, 'one publicly approved standard of service, irrespective of income, class or race, replaced the double standard which invariably meant second-class services for second-class citizens.'[14] And here an important reason for equality of treatment and the resultant integration despite other class distinctions is to be found on the side of demand, not simply supply: 'The middle-classes, invited to enter the Service in 1948, did so and have since largely stayed with the Service. They have not contracted out of socialized medical care as they have done in other fields like secondary education and retirement pensions.'[15]

It is important for the upper and middle classes to share in the benefits as well as the costs of welfare if the welfare state itself is not to acquire the stigma of catering mainly for the needs of the lower classes. Any *de facto* absence of universality may encourage redistribution but it impedes integration. Besides that, the use of the National Health Service, if it is felt mainly to be the resort of the poor and the indigent, may spoil the image of themselves held by the needy. They may come to think of themselves as lazy and inferior, and separated by a class barrier from the more fortunate members of the population.[16] The mass media have a social obligation to propagandize in favour of the Service and show how it is being used by all groups in the community. Unfortunately, a critical stance towards the welfare state is more often to be found,[17] and this has the same effect as a means test in contributing to the process of stigmatization and self-stigmatization.

Third, the National Health Service reaches the hard-to-reach whom private profit-maximizers would in any case exclude from the world of welfare. In this way the pathological cases too are integrated, via equality of access, rights and treatment, into the community of which they are a part.

The problem is that many of the most needy in modern society are precisely those people with not only unmet but unexpressed needs, to be found notably 'among the poor, the badly educated, the old, those living alone and other handicapped groups. Their needs are not expressed and not met because of ignorance, inertia, fear, difficulties of making contact with the services, failures of co-ordination and co-operation between services, and for other reasons. These are the people – and there are substantial numbers of them in all populations – who are difficult to reach. Yet they are often the people with the greatest needs.'[18]

A welfare state with universalist services eliminates the stigma and shame that might frighten potential customers away from public services; and the fact that the services are free on demand to all means that there is no financial barrier to proper treatment and also that the hard-to-reach will be integrated at treatment centres with a typical cross-section of the community in terms of class, race, age-group, marital status and other characteristics.

Moreover, since not all needs are 'felt' needs, a welfare state often makes potential consumers aware of needs and also of the existence of services to which they are entitled and which will mitigate or remove the needs. Thus a general practitioner conducting a routine examination might diagnose an unmet need which cannot be articulated or self-diagnosed (such as malnutrition, or the need for mental health services). And a social worker dealing with problem A in the social security offices or in the client's home might notice problem B, inform the potential patient of his rights to a service, and reassure him that he can apply without fear of being reprimanded for wasting the professionals' time. The emphasis in the modern welfare state is on rights, not deterrence; on letting the needy in, not keeping them out. In such a system, the social worker has an educative as well as an administrative function to perform: 'Education, as distinct from propaganda, is about freedom; it increases awareness of possible choices. To enable clients better to exercise choice is an integral part of the functions of social work and here, it may be said, the social worker as an individual enacts an educational role which is sanctioned as such by society.'[19]

As an example of that educational role, consider the case of blindness prevented. In the period from 1948 to 1962, the National Assistance Board (not the medical profession) was the principal source of referral for preventive action against blindness among the aged. These people were hard to reach but had to come in for cash benefits because even now 'it is possible to see two nations in old age; greater inequalities in living standards after work than in work.'[20] Having nothing but their state pensions to live on, they applied for national assistance; and helpful clerks then advised them to take advantage of their right to another service, a free eye-test.

Often the hard-to-reach have multiple needs, so personal contact is invaluable. Such a personal relationship (and not just a formal 'paper relationship') 'can be the source of knowledge and information, advice and encouragement. It is also a source of freedom. Blindness prevented is an enlargement of freedom.'[21]

There is no substitute for human contact, and thus Professor Titmuss rejected mechanical solutions to the problems of the dependent (such as the negative income tax) on the grounds that they are impersonal: 'Instead of the home visit and personal contact with a caseworker there will be substituted the postal application, the computer and the postal payment.'[22] Personal contact is desirable in itself (even the alienation and revolt of students may be traced back in part to neglect of teaching and lack of human communication on the part of professors); and it also allows the social worker to contact the hard-to-reach (his education-disseminating function) and to identify fundamental social shortcomings (his information-gathering function).

Universalism in the social services means provision of benefits as of right; but automatic and non-judgemental administration should not be allowed to reduce opportunities for human contact. Again, where benefits are selective, precision of rules should be accompanied by a measure of discretion on the part of the authorities in order to ensure 'individualized justice'.[23] Such a mixed model is not only more humane but more flexible than one based on rules alone, and avoids the rigid 'pathology of "legalism"' implicit in an overcodified system 'based on precedent and responsive only very slowly to rapidly changing human needs and circumstances'.[24]

In Britain, the Supplementary Benefits Commission is a good illustration of the mixed model Titmuss had in mind. It values precision, and has published leaflets, booklets and handbooks to explain the rules it applies and thus to advise the citizen of his rights. At the same time, however, it also sees a role for discretion and believes in leaving scope for 'flexible responses to human needs and to an immense variety of complex individual circumstances'.[25] Naturally, abuse of power should be prevented, and there must be checks on 'the interfering, moralising, judgemental caseworker'.[26] People should be informed of their rights and adequate appeal mechanisms should be provided. Provision too should be made for sensitive quality controls on discretion via audits and inspections, collection of statistics, surveys, research, response to constructive criticism of performance from outside individuals and organizations, and improved training of staff. The present system has the disadvantage that A passes a moral judgement on B as a precondition for discretionary redistributive benefits (a disadvantage since, after all, human decision-makers can be biased and fallible); but a check on that power is provided by the fact that the official may be asked to justify his behaviour to a superior or to an appeals tribunal with greater sensitivity to current social values.

The present system, because it allows for personal contact at a number of points in the welfare state, helps to ensure more adequate participation by the hard-to-reach. Understandably, this increases pressure on resources in the same way as does the provision of benefits as of right with the minimum of stigmatizing rules and regulations. But many of the needs experienced by the hard-to-reach are diswelfares imposed by social change; and social integration is in any case as legitimate an end in its own right as, say, the self-seeking profit maximization of the private entrepreneur.

Fourth, there is the example of altruistic, voluntary gifts to strangers. This to Titmuss is an important index of social health, and also a paradigm of what social policy is all about: 'The grant, or the gift or unilateral transfer – whether it takes the form of cash, time, energy, satisfaction, blood or even life itself – is the distinguishing mark of the social (in policy and administration) just as exchange or bilateral transfer is the mark of the economic.'[27] Through the act of giving, the individual expresses his involvement in, and commitment to, the community, and thus strengthens the cultural bonds of the group.

As an example of the unilateral transfer Titmuss takes blood donorship and transfusion. This he believes to be a 'sensitive universal social indicator'[28] or index of the cultural values and quality of human relationships prevalent in a particular society, as may be seen from a comparison of systems relying on paid donors with systems relying on unpaid donors.

One of the greatest social costs of the private market system is the introduction of the cash nexus, the economist's *quid pro quo*, the 'dialectic of hedonism'[29] into relationships between citizens. The paid donor sells his blood for what the market will bear, and regards the transaction as impersonal and mechanical, as no less commercial than any other way of earning money (to which the sale of blood may be an alternative or a supplement). The possessive individualism of the utilitarian market-place thus stifles the spirit of giving, drives out community-spiritedness, and undermines the quality of social relationships and values.

Material acquisitiveness has supplanted the spirit of fellowship in both the United States and Russia, as the index of blood donorship patterns demonstrates. In the United States, paid donors are not typical of the population, and the blood donorship is biased towards low-income groups, the black, the male, the young, the unskilled, the unemployed, the deprived, the socially inadequate. These constitute a 'blood proletariat'[30] supplying blood to those classes who can afford to pay. Such bifurcation indicates that the cash incentive is simply incompatible with the sense of community. And in Russia too the sense of community must be low, since Soviet donors must be bribed to give blood by the promise of longer holidays, free public transport for up to a month, days off, free meals, and even the exceptionally high price of 60 roubles per litre (equivalent to, say, half a month's pay at the national minimum wage).[31] Such attractive conditions are indicative of the scarcity of blood for transfusion in the Soviet Union, but also of the low social priority of mutual aid. In both the United States and Russia, if blood is a good index, we may expect alienation from the community and ethical decay to result from the low sense of social integration: 'Although attempts have been made to value human life, no money values can be attached to the presence or absence of a spirit of altruism in a society. Altruism in giving to a stranger does not begin and end with blood donations. It may touch every aspect of life and affect the whole fabric of values.'[32]

Consider now Britain, where there are virtually no material rewards in money or kind to blood donors and where blood is a free gift to unnamed strangers. In Britain, unlike the United States, the blood donorship appears broadly typical of the national population in respect of age (up to 55), sex (after allowing for the effects of child-bearing on younger women's participation rates) and marital status (even the divorced, widowed and separated are not alienated from the group and contribute their due proportions along with the married and the single, giving indeed if anything slightly more often than their numbers in the national population would have led one to expect).[33] As for social class, there may be some over-representation of social classes I and II and a corresponding under-representation of the lower classes, but this is indicative not of alienation but of the presence of additional variables in the social welfare equation (variables such as the higher percentage of non-eligibles among lower income groups; or the practice in institutional sessions of giving executives and white-collar workers the first chance to volunteer, so that the list may well be closed before the men on the shop-floor get an opportunity to donate).[34] Titmuss based his conclusions on a small-sample pilot survey of some 3813 donors in England and Wales conducted in 1967; and it is worthwhile noting that as many as 13% of donor-households studied revealed incomes of the chief earner such that they might have been at or even below the Supplementary Benefits level.[35] So much for the estrangement of the poor!

As far as donor-motivation is concerned, Titmuss was convinced that at least 80% of the answers received in his 1967 questionnaire survey suggested 'a high sense of social responsibility towards the needs of other members of society'.[36] The reasons given by donors to explain their free gift included pure altruism (a desire to contribute to the welfare of others in need), social awareness (a thank-offering for previous transfusions received by oneself or a member of one's family from unknown strangers; or in case one might in future need such gifts), awareness of need, sense of duty (a feeling one *ought* to help others), or response to an appeal from a workmate or on the radio. Clearly, such people felt integrated in the community: they could have contracted out of the cost without contracting out of the potential benefit (and the ideology of the private market teaches us to give as little and take as much as we can), but they did not. They believed in 'man's biological need for social relations': 'To the philosopher's question "what kind of actions ought we to perform?" they replied, in effect, "those which will cause more good to exist in the universe than there would otherwise be if we did not so act".'[37]

One of the reasons for the successful public response in Britain to the National Blood Transfusion Service is that it operates together with the National Health Service, and both embody the same values. The 1948 system is vital insofar as it provides an institutional structure that allows for the expression of altruism: 'The most unsordid act of British social policy in the twentieth century has allowed and encouraged sentiments of altruism, reciprocity and social duty to express themselves; to be made explicit and identifiable in measureable patterns of behaviour by all social groups and classes. In part this is attributable to the fact that, structurally and functionally, the Health Service is not socially divisive; its universal and free access basis has contributed much, we believe, to the social liberties of the subject in allowing people the choice to give or not to give blood for unseen strangers.'[38]

There are two points to note here which concern integration and involvement. Firstly, both the National Health Service and the National Blood Transfusion Service make the assumption of universality of need, and the further assumption that the donor will willingly forego the right to prescribe the characteristics of the recipient. Blood donation is not tied in the United Kingdom, and there is no 'prescribed and specified discrimination in the destination of the gift. One of the principles of the National Blood Transfusion Service and the National Health Service is to provide services on the basis of common human needs; there must be no allocation of resources which could create a sense of separateness between people. It is the explicit or implicit institutionalization of separateness, whether categorized in terms of income, class, race, colour or religion, rather than the recognition of the similarities between people and their needs which causes much of the world's suffering.'[39] The success of the system in stimulating individual volunteers to make free gifts to unnamed strangers demonstrates how far donors share the values of the Services. Symbolic of the network of interdependence and mutual aid that exists in modern Britain is the British haemophiliac, a person who relies annually on the free gifts of up to fifty unnamed citizens and is likely to have in his veins at any one time the blood of rich and poor, black and white, male and female. Blood and life are emotive areas; but so are integration and money.

2) Secondly, the structural arrangements in Britain help to further integration and altruism not only because the donor is not paid but because the recipient is not expected to pay. Perhaps man has 'a biological need to help',[40] but he will be reluctant to satisfy it by donating blood which will then be sold at a price set by supply and demand to a private patient. This restricts his freedom of choice (and specifically his freedom to donate), since the opportunity 'to exercise a moral choice to give in non-monetary forms to strangers' is an 'essential human right'.[41] Certainly, without the existence of the National Health Service, men 'in the relatively affluent, acquisitive and divisive societies of the twentieth century'[42] would be less willing to give to strangers (persons outside the circle of family and friends) rather than sell to them. It is important to remember that in some circumstances the cash payment can be a disincentive (since 'altruistic donors can hardly be expected to give their blood to profit-making hospitals,'[43] and might refrain altogether from donation); and that in all cases it erodes the sense of inclusion and community which a group has the right to choose.

We have seen that paid-donorship and voluntary-donorship systems are indices of quite different social climates. It is possible, however, that the gap between them can conceptually be narrowed by drawing a parallel between free gifts in Western society and the ritual exchange of gifts in the primitive societies described by Mauss and Lévi-Strauss.[44] In the ritual exchange system the gift is neither a profit-motivated economic transaction nor a totally disinterested unilateral transfer. Rather, it is a moral nexus, 'bringing about and maintaining personal relationships between individuals and groups'.[45] Gift leads to counter-gift (so that to give is also to receive, albeit possibly after a time-lag) or at least to a thank-you; and there are social sanctions such as shame if one refuses to give.

Upon inspection, however, it becomes clear that there is only one real similarity between gifts in primitive society and the gift of blood in Britain, namely that in both cases the transaction is anchored deeply in the social fabric and cultural orientation of the collectivity. Otherwise, attitudes to 'friendship and intercourse' diverge. There is in Britain, for example, no social obligation or compulsion to give blood, no reward for donating nor any social sanctions (not even moral re-crimination) for not doing so. There is in Britain no personal expression of gratitude (due to the anonymity of donor and recipient and the absence of the personal face-to-face confrontation we would find in a small-scale society). Nor is there even a guarantee that the gift of blood will lead to a future counter-gift (one hopes that one will never need a blood transfusion and has no certainty that others will in future provide the gift, or indeed that there will continue to be a National Health Service).

Of course, even in Britain the counter-gift is implicit. For one thing, the very act of donation yields pleasure to the donors because they are able to transcend self-love and demonstrate their attachment to the group: 'To "love" themselves they recognized the need to "love" strangers,'[46] and hence they elect to make gifts with no economic or exchange value. Again (and this is a more sociological factor than self-felicitation), although the donors neither desire nor expect a return gift, they know that they or their family may one day be dependent on such reciprocation, and this reinforces their awareness of interdependence and their sense of integration. Men willing to provide blood are likely to be men confident that others will provide them with a similar gift if needed, and thus men confident as to the moral health of their community: 'In not asking for or expecting any payment of money these donors signified their belief in the willingness of other men to act altruistically in the future, and to combine together to make a gift freely available should they have a need for it. By expressing confidence in the behaviour of future unknown strangers they were thus denying the Hobbesian thesis that men are devoid of any distinctively moral sense.'[47]

Blood donation is not the only possible index of 'creative altruism' ('creative in the sense that the self is realized with the help of anonymous others').[48] Consider, for example, the case of teaching hospitals: 'To qualify as a doctor in Britain, it is probable that the average medical student now needs access to or contact with in one form or another some 300 different patients.'[49] These patients are, because of the universality of the National Health system, drawn from all sectors of the population (whereas American doctors train and do research on the indigent, with the curious implication that, the fewer indigent there are today, the fewer doctors there will be tomorrow). The patients are strangers but their willingness to act as specimens is nonetheless 'taken for granted in the name of research, the advancement of medical science, society's need for doctors, the better training and more rapid progression of doctors professionally and financially and, ultimately, for the good of all patients irrespective of race, religion, colour or territory'.[50]

Here we have a case where the doctor (as student and researcher) and the community clearly benefit, but where the patient in the

short run does not (except insofar as the latent function of his helpfulness is that he in practice benefits from more medical contact).
Typically, the benefits accrue in the long run and probably 'further the
well-being of some future collectivity of patients. If old age pensioners
with chronic bronchitis put to themselves the Hobbesian question – why
should men do other than act to their own immediate advantage? –
they might start charging for the gifts they make which are more likely
to benefit future cohorts of chronic bronchitics.'[51] Yet pensioners do
not charge for the gifts they make, and acknowledge their social
obligation and sense of integration into the community by making a
disinterested unilateral transfer. They thus identify themselves as
members of the 'caring community', which also includes co-operative
field and control material used by sociologists, laboratory volunteers
used by psychologists, the mentally ill used by student psychiatrists,
schoolchildren used by student teachers, and so on. This willingness to
serve the community without a reciprocal return gift in the short run is
not only a sign of integration but is indispensable to progress: 'More
and more instruments of social policy are in action requiring, as
scientific knowledge advances *pari passu* with professionalization,
these acts of "voluntaryism" which carry with them no wish for return
acts or return gifts.'[52] Pity the professional in a society where free gifts
have become articles of commerce, since science and technology have
increased rather than decreased the need for altruism.

Were free gifts to become mere commercial consumption goods to
be bought and sold like any others, there would be no justification for
not replacing all welfare services (schools, hospitals, social work, and
even universities and churches) by private individualistic markets
which would accord so much better with the erosion of community.
The choice of the market would set men free from 'the conscience of
obligation',[53] and social policy would become economic policy.
Fortunately, however, that sad point has not yet been reached. Social
policy still exists because free gifts still exist, because there is still a
premium on integration and involvement.

9 Universalism III: Planned Redistribution

Redistributive policies are operated by the political authorities when they interfere with the pattern of claims of command-over-resources-over-time as set by the market and 'assign claims from one set of people who are said to produce or earn the national product to another set of people who may merit compassion and charity but not economic rewards for productive service'.[1] The idea is that the government both imposes costs (in the form of taxes) and provides benefits (in cash or in kind); and that redistribution occurs when the money claimed in taxes is not restored in precisely the same measure in the form of benefits to precisely those taxpayers who provided it, but is redirected instead from one person or group to another person or group.

All welfare schemes are redistributive, and neutrality is not a feasible objective: 'I do not know of any programmes in any country of the world which do not, in their total effects, increase or decrease inequalities in the distribution of incomes and life chances. Some benefit the rich more than the poor; others benefit the poor more than the rich.'[2] The real problem is therefore not to establish that redistribution is taking place but to identify the direction and magnitude of that redistribution, and possibly take steps to plan it.

It is often asserted that the British welfare state is redistributive from the rich to the poor, and even that the burden is so excessive that the well-to-do are in danger of impoverishment. It is widely believed that taxes in Britain fall disproportionately on the well-off, while the expansion of the social services disproportionately favours the lower income groups. Titmuss, however, while acknowledging the egalitarian aims of the welfare state, was not convinced that greater equality was in fact being attained. Writing in 1964, he announced bluntly that 'the advent of "The Welfare State" in Britain after the

Second World War has not led to any significant redistribution of income and wealth in favour of the poorer classes.'[3] At the very most, the welfare state had prevented existing gaps from widening in the post-war period: 'Had social policies been less influential during these years ..... then, I believe, the trend towards inequality would have been more marked.'[4] The reasons for the modest net impact of the welfare state will become clear if we examine them first from the point of view of costs and then from the point of view of benefits.

Consider first costs. Here Titmuss pointed out that the tax system may be seen in certain circumstances not as a burden but as a form of welfare. Deductions and tax allowances for life assurance, pension schemes, dependent children, mortgage interest, or maintenance to a former wife may be a form of social engineering, but they are also a form of collective provision. Such tax saving is analogous to a transfer payment, since it increases the taxpayer's net disposable income at the expense of the rest of the community; and in that sense fiscal welfare is similar to social welfare.

Fiscal welfare often rewards rather than penalizes the well-to-do. Allowances, for example, being lump-sum, are clearly more valuable the higher one moves up the tax scale, and may move a man out of higher tax ranges altogether (thereby reducing the bite of progressive income tax). At the other end of the scale, however, they are valueless to low-income families who pay zero direct tax (and whose needs might be acute where they are not only poor in income but rich in offspring). Hence it might cost the Exchequer more to allow a man paying progressive income tax at the highest rates to deduct mortgage interest from his gross income than to provide him directly with a modest council flat. Or consider the case of private pension schemes, which (as a deduction for tax purposes) represent a substantial opportunity cost to the Treasury (and hence hidden subsidy from society): 'As at present organized, the cost to the Treasury (the whole community) of private pension schemes substantially exceeds the Treasury contribution to social security pensions for the whole population. The pensions of the rich are more heavily subsidized by the community than the pensions of the poor.'[5]

One of the reasons for the continued preponderance of middle- and upper-class students in higher education (one of the higher cost sectors of the welfare state) has been the existence of a prosperous private market in secondary education; and this private market has in turn been heavily subsidized by the state through the system of fiscal welfare. For one thing, independent schools often enjoy partial charity status for purposes of taxation. Moreover, a father is allowed a tax deduction for each child in full-time education regardless of the rate of tax paid or whether or not the child is in receipt of a scholarship. And again, a man may finance his son's education at a public school by covenanting. Here, since part of the father's income is automatically alienated and transferred to someone else (such as the infant), so is the liability to pay tax on it, a considerable advantage if the recipient has no income of his own. For example: 'A married man with an income of £15,350 a year can put fully £250 in the hands of his aged and impoverished mother-in-law at a personal cost to himself of £28 2s. 6d.'[6] Clearly, in the case of an educational covenant, this represents a substantial subsidy by the taxpayer to privilege, élitism, a class monopoly of graduate jobs, and even ultimately marriage between two fortunes.

In the case of the deductibles we have been considering, fiscal welfare is unambiguously redistributive. It alters the pattern of claims that would otherwise have obtained in the market, and not necessarily towards those most in need of help. This suggests that a closer examination of the social effects of the tax system is needed than has been provided by those economists who have concluded, after examining Inland Revenue statistics over time, that income differentials are narrowing. It is not clear that progressive taxation is leading to greater equality for the simple reason that existing statistics are misleading and ignore three important difficulties:

First, Inland Revenue statistics and studies based on them are lifeless and unconvincing since they do not adequately take social change into account. An increasing propensity for wives to work will, for example, mean increasing inequality of incomes in a country where husband and wife are assessed together for income tax purposes (although, sociologically speaking, it actually means greater equality of incomes in society, as would be apparent if they were assessed separately). Again, if incomes are aggregated and more working-class wives go out to work while more middle-class wives stay at home, the income distribution table will look more egalitarian for spurious reasons unconnected with progressive income tax (indeed, the statistical equalization of incomes might actually conceal a situation where life had become proportionately easier for middle-class families and proportionately harder for the poor, thus forcing lower-class wives to take on extra work outside the home). And early marriage too may give the impression of greater equality, since many low-paid young girls thereby disappear from the income tax statistics (some of them reappearing later, of course, to inflate aggregated figures for low-paid married couples). Finally, full employment may reduce inequality by converting the unemployed into the low-paid and thereby boosting their incomes. These examples show us that, here as elsewhere, statistics are meaningless by themselves and must first be integrated into the general sociological context. That done, greater equality of incomes could well turn out to be a statistical mirage.

Second, studies of inequality have concentrated on the individual, not the kinship group. Yet clearly, although the individual may be the earner, the family is likely to be the spender; and thus, although the husband, wife and dependent children may be assessed separately for tax (so long as there is not compulsory aggregation of family incomes), they are likely to spend collectively.

Statistics are misleading since, despite the appearance on paper of a movement towards greater equality of pre-tax incomes, the family might still have the same funds, simply shared among more individuals. Such sharing of income might take the form of covenants transferring income to deprived earners who pay tax at a lower rate. Thus, for example, 'a wealthy taxpayer with a separated wife, a mistress and four children (all with "separate" incomes under different schedules) might be represented in the Board's yearly tables by six or seven income units'.[7] Alternatively, sharing of income might take the form of the 'one man company', created by a kinship group. Here one big salary (say, of an actor) is paid into the company, whose salaried directors are the earner's wife and children (all claiming a personal allowance against tax). They vote to pay the earner a salary on a modest scale (while retaining the rest of his income as capital) and then ask him to spend their earnings for them along with his own. In this way progressive income tax at higher rates is avoided and statistical data are made impure via the transference of income from one person to another.

Third, studies of inequality have tended to focus on income differentials, not on capital. Yet property (especially inherited property) can be a source of great inequality, and hence a meaningful study ought to take into account the effects of accumulated rights and claims. The existence of family and educational trusts, for example, or of stored-up wealth will affect command-over-resources-over-time as much (or more) in several generations as they do now, and in that sense they benefit the unborn as well as the living. Clearly, a meaningful investigation ought to take a time-period much longer than simply the current fiscal year.

Studies should be made not just of the distribution of property but of the extent to which income can be and is being converted into wealth. A covenant can transform income into capital, as in the case where the beneficiary receives a lump-sum at marriage or age 21 (a lump-sum which is tax-free since the beneficiary has already been taxed on it, although not his older, richer father who would have paid at a higher rate). Moreover, an executive may accept a lower salary while working in exchange for a tax-free lump-sum on retirement; or ask for a lump-sum masquerading as compensation for loss of office due to a fictitious or contrived redundancy (in which case the additional remuneration is not only a tax-free benefit for the recipient but also a deductible expense for the company that pays it). Such opportunities to convert taxable income into tax-free capital reduce the gradient of progressive taxation, and mean that more attention must be paid to the concept of wealth and the resultant inheritable status.

Thus, in conclusion, it is natural to wonder if the tax system is really as great a burden on the rich as has often been supposed. Instruments such as covenants (which avoid both income tax and death duties) represent a substantial loss of revenue to the Exchequer and not all classes are in a position to benefit equally from them. Besides that, the rich are more likely to have the knowledge, expertise and opportunity to spread incomes evenly over time than are the lower classes, and are thereby more able to frustrate the egalitarian objectives of progressive taxation.

Such considerations lead inescapably to the question of whether inequality is today more of a problem or less of a problem than it was, say, before the Second World War. To this there is no clear answer. All that is clear is that we in fact know very little about the changing distribution of income and wealth, and that more study should be devoted to relative (quite apart from absolute) deprivation,[8] and to the 'concealed multipliers of inequality'[9] that still exist in our economic and social institutions. Concern with inequality, Titmuss stressed, is not *passé*.

Let us turn now from the redistributive effects of the costs of welfare to the redistributive effects of benefits, and here again we must ask ourselves the key question: 'Whose welfare state?' It is important to know who benefits from government expenditures on welfare. To many, however, the truth will come as a surprise: 'The major beneficiaries of the high-cost sectors of social welfare are the middle and upper income classes. The poor make more use of certain services (for instance, public assistance) but these tend on a *per capita* basis to be the low-cost sectors.'[10]

In the case of the universities, for example, the 'major beneficiaries' are clearly not the children of coloured immigrants or manual labourers: 'Today 45 per cent of children from higher income and professional families are admitted to full-time degree courses at universities and their equivalent, compared with 10 per cent of those from homes where the father is in a clerical job, right down to 4 per cent where he is a skilled worker, and 2 per cent where he is a semi-skilled or unskilled worker.... What is perhaps less well known is how remarkably persistent the inequalities in Britain have remained over the last ten to twenty years; the years of "The Welfare State" .... In point of fact, the relative chances of getting to university for working-class and middle-class children have changed little over the last quarter of a century.'[11] Those who have benefited most thus appear to be those who would probably have benefited most in any case. This has great disadvantages:

For one thing, rather than automatically increasing social mobility and integration, such an educational system may actually provide reinforcement to birth by making inequality seem even more the result of natural attributes and innate ability: 'The weight of evidence shows that in most European countries it has been one of the most powerful forces of social conservatism, giving the appearance of legitimacy to social inequalities by treating "a social attribute as a natural attribute".'[12] It thus has the ideological function of validating the social *status quo*.

Moreover, rather than narrowing pay differentials, the educational system is likely to increase them. After all, education may have social and intellectual rewards, but it also has value 'as a straight-forward commercial investment': 'The return on higher education as a purely commercial investment for the individual is probably larger today in most Western countries than any other form of investment. If heavily financed by the State, and if proportionately more children from better-off homes benefit, then the system will be redistributive in favour of the rich.'[13] It is true that the working-class school-leaver may be earning good money at a time when the university student is struggling to survive on a grant (to which the school-leaver contributes, of course, through his taxes). Later in life, however, the graduate may be 'twenty times or more better off' than the school-leaver, 'measured solely in terms of annual cash income, with less disabling disease, a longer expectation of life, a lower age of retirement, more inherited wealth, a proportionately greater and more assured pension, a tax free lump sum perhaps one hundred times larger, and in receipt of substantially more non-wage income and amenities in forms that escape income tax, being neither money nor convertible into money.'[14]

Clearly, the welfare state, via the existing university system, is not helping to reduce either class inequalities (which may indeed become sharper once birth and property are reinforced in the minds of men by cultural formation) or earnings differentials (which are likely to become larger as a premium on specialization and training). Rather, the university system is itself becoming a pillar of inequality, operating with the rationalization that economic growth necessitates more division of labour and more specialized training: 'As industrial, scientific and technological development demands more people with higher education there will be, as in Britain, pressures to invest more scarce resources in such education at the expense of education for the masses, and also to concentrate secondary education on those who will go on to higher education. These pressures, we must recognize, are growing stronger in our societies.'[15]

Such pressures are dangerous since they are a threat to social cohesion: 'These processes, necessary as they are, tend on balance to generate disequalizing forces and, by demanding higher standards of education, training and acquired skills, they can make more difficult the task of integrating people with different cultural backgrounds and levels of motivation. While we may raise expectations in people's minds about what the future may hold, technology simultaneously raises the barriers to entry. This process, now becoming known in the U.S.A. as "credentialism", is believed to be partly responsible for the solidifying of a permanent underclass of deprived citizens, un-educated, unattached and alternating between apathetic resignation and frustrated violence.'[16]

As a second illustration of the proposition that 'the major bene-ficiaries of the high-cost sectors of social welfare are the middle and upper income classes,' consider the experience of the National Health Service, where equality of access and availability has not meant equality of utilization: 'We have learnt from fifteen years experience of the Health Service that the higher income groups know how to make better use of the Service; they tend to receive more specialist attention; occupy more of the beds in better equipped and staffed hospitals; receive more elective surgery; have better maternity care, and are more likely to get psychiatric help and psychotherapy than low income groups – particularly the unskilled.'[17] As evidence that the well-to-do often have higher medical consultation rates than manual labourers (especially agricultural labourers), note that eye-tests and dental treatment are proportionately more in demand in prosperous residential and commercial areas;[18] and also that even under the free National Health Service the higher social classes appear to have received proportionately more blood transfusions than the semi-skilled and the unskilled who constitute social classes IV and V.[19] The latter is a surprising result as the incidence of morbidity and mortality is actually *higher* among the lower income groups; and reflects the fact that the middle classes have received proportionately more surgery and other medical treatment necessitating a transfusion.

Naturally, the well-to-do have as much of a right as anyone else to the free-on-demand, as-of-right universalist services of the welfare state. The point is simply that their share of benefits has been more than proportionate to their numbers in the population (although all beneficiaries of course receive the same service once it is actually provided): 'Middle-income groups make more and better use of all services; they are more articulate and more demanding. They have learnt better in all countries how to find their way around a complicated welfare world.'[20] This is not a criticism. On the contrary, it is good that the middle classes know their rights and insist on proper treatment. It remains, however, a sad fact that the hard-to-reach and even the unskilled do not have the same awareness and hence do not enjoy the same facilities (to which they, in the modern welfare state, have the same rights).

There is a further point on the side of benefits, namely that the higher income groups tend to enjoy more complementary benefits than the lower income groups. These complementary welfare benefits (which Titmuss calls 'occupational welfare', to distinguish them from 'fiscal welfare' and 'social welfare') are provided by firms to employees on the basis of achieved status and employment record. Such fringe benefits may take the form of a company car, a flat at a token rental, business trips abroad with rooms in first-class hotels and visits (with clients, of course) to expensive night clubs and restaurants, or even golf lessons. The firm may provide an occupational pension for the employee and his wife (possibly offering a higher non-contributory pension in exchange for a lower current salary as, while the pension will ultimately be taxable, it will be less than salary and hence taxed at a lower rate); death benefits; child allowances or payment of school fees at private schools for the children of key employees (possibly via educational covenants made in favour of the child, who can then recover tax); medical and health services; redundancy payments; tax-free lump-sums upon retirement; and other benefits in cash and kind. The list is a long one, and it is no surprise to learn that occupational welfare may well have the effect of doubling the standard of living of recipients.[21]

In practice, these benefits have the same function as the benefits associated with social welfare: 'A substantial part of all these multifarious benefits can be interpreted as the recognition of dependencies; the dependencies of old age, of sickness and incapacity, of childhood, widowhood and so forth. They are in effect, if not in administrative method, "social services", duplicating and overlapping social and fiscal welfare benefits.'[22] Occupational welfare benefits are, however, not without their disadvantages:

First, occupational welfare, unlike modern British social welfare, is selectivist. It thus nourishes privilege (by favouring white-collar workers and the middle classes) and promotes inequality (by increasing the gap between those with occupational benefits and those without). Occupational welfare, being divisive rather than unifying and integrative, weakens social loyalties and attachment to the community.

Second, occupational welfare has the function of consolidating the interests of employer and employee (most visibly perhaps in the case of cheap stock options for executives). It thus contributes not just to good human relations in industry but to the creation of powerful pressure groups and a new corporate state. After all, occupational welfare is 'mostly contingent welfare; the undivided loyalty tranquillizer of the corporation; the basis of a new monolithic society'.[23] In that sense occupational welfare reinforces the power of the corporation in society in the same way as the communion and the confessional reinforced the power of the medieval Church.

Third, occupational pension rights and other kinds of occupational welfare may be forfeited by redundancy or change of job, and are hence an obstacle to mobility. Titmuss warned that 'a gradual hardening in the economic arteries of the nation' could in this way result: 'These new laws of settlement may, in time, constitute impediments to change as formidable in their own way as the laws which Adam Smith indicted in 1776.'[24] Perhaps the British white-collar worker already feels as trapped as the Mauritian labourer who has moved into a 'camp' of tied cottages on a sugar estate: 'In their efforts to attract labour, some of the estates have taken considerable trouble to make these camps as attractive as possible, with playing fields and meeting halls. Nevertheless, the unwillingness of workers to live on the estates is understandable because of the loss of freedom involved in being tied to one employer.'[25]

Fourth, not only is occupational welfare an unhealthy system of provision from the point of view of society, but it is, ironically enough, paid for in part by the community as a whole. Because they are tax-deductibles to the firm, about one-half the cost of occupational welfare benefits in Britain (assuming a rate of corporation tax of about 50%) falls on the general body of taxpayers in the form of revenue foregone by the Exchequer. The burden is even greater if all or part of the cost is passed on to the consumer of the commodity produced by the firm in the form of higher prices (an anti-social and regressive technique for financing welfare projects). Of course, some occupational welfare benefits are taxed once they are in the hands of the recipient; but then not all, and seldom at true market value. And even if the recipient were to be charged the full cost of the benefit, he would in fact be paying tax only on income he might have spent, not on income he might have earned. Yet since the benefit is given to him in lieu of a far higher gross salary, income tax (possibly at higher rates) is avoided, the gradient of progressive taxation reduced, and the general body of taxpayers cheated. Most occupational welfare benefits are thus indubitably a cloak for additional net remuneration going to those who need it least.

In summary, then, occupational welfare needs to be integrated with fiscal and social welfare if our present-day welfare system (made up as it is of three redistributive sub-systems, each of which alters the pattern of claims on current and future resources) is to work in the national interest. And, to be honest, the welfare system is not in all respects working in the national interest at the moment: taking into account all three sub-systems of welfare (i.e. not neglecting fiscal and occupational welfare, the two 'submerged parts of the "Iceberg of Social Policy" '[26]), it is clear that, 'as at present organized, they are simultaneously enlarging and consolidating the area of social inequality.'[27]

Thus, although the existence of social welfare has made the trend towards inequality less marked than it would otherwise have been, many gaps still remain in the welfare state. The tax-burden has been less progressive than is often supposed, and the social services have not in practice favoured all equally but favoured the well-to-do proportionately more: 'Take, for example, the case of two fathers each with two children, one earning $60,000 a year, the other $1,500 a year. In combining the effect of direct social welfare expenditures for children and indirect fiscal welfare expenditures for children the result is that the rich father now gets thirteen times more from the State in recognition of the dependent needs of childhood.'[28] Such differential treatment of different groups in the population indicates where the real challenge for the future is to be found.

The challenge must be met by selective discrimination. If welfare is really to redistribute life-chances, then it must by its very nature become selective and strive 'to discriminate positively with the minimum risk of stigma, in favour of those whose needs are greatest.'[29] A society which wishes to use its social services as a means of 'equalizing opportunities for people in unequal circumstances'[30] must recognize that proportionately more resources must be diverted to the socially disadvantaged than to more normal groups in the population if true equality of opportunity is to be established. There should, in other words, be a greater emphasis on 'community responsibility' and 'social growth', of which the following are quantifiable social indicators: 'When our societies are spending proportionately more on the educationally deprived than on the educationally normal; when the rehousing of the poor is proceeding at a greater rate than the rehousing of the middle classes; when proportionately more medical care is being devoted to the needs of the long-term chronically sick than to those of the average sick; when more social workers are moving into public programmes than into private child guidance clinics; when there are smaller differentials in incomes and assets between rich and poor, coloured and pink families.'[31]

Greater equality of opportunity is highly desirable from the point of view of the community. For one thing, social growth is not antithetical to economic growth, but may be complementary to it: 'More equality in income and wealth, education, and the enjoyment of the decencies of social living might conceivably be a democratic pre-condition of faster economic growth.'[32] And again, equality of access to classless services fosters a sense of integration. Morale in wartime Britain, for example, was considerably improved by 'an equitable sharing-out of food, shelter and social services:'[33] 'Self-control was easier when there was no awareness of injustice arising from the way in which the primary wants were met. The knowledge that large numbers of those who were privileged in the community were also carrying on with their work and facing the risks that ordinary people faced, the knowledge that such facilities as the evacuation and shelter schemes were available and were not limited to particular groups – here were important foundations of morale.'[34]

Clearly 'there is a problem (as there has always been) of priorities in the allocation of scarce resources in the social policy field.'[35] Yet, precisely because the existence of scarcity imposes the constraint of choice, it is important that priorities be set by socially determined criteria and that conscious decision replace accident of birth or fortune. Titmuss believed that the community ought to identify those whose state of dependency is most acute (and who will probably turn out to be the poor, the sick, the handicapped, the coloured, the educationally deprived, the badly housed) and to skew the distribution of the community's wealth towards them, since their needs are greatest: 'To me, the "Welfare State" has no meaning unless it is positively and constructively concerned with redistributive justice and social participation.'[36] Understandably, of course, if one person is to be given a larger share in command-over-resources by the state, another must accept a smaller part. Thus if, for example, 'we are to plan for the aged to have a larger share of the National Income then we are, in effect, planning for others to have less.'[37] One man's welfare could well be another man's ill-fare. Fortunately, however, consensus replaces conflict: 'It is now widely accepted that in all sectors of the economy there is a national need to diminish both the absolute fact and the psychological sense of social and economic discrimination.'[38] The community recognizes the need for greater equality of opportunity and increased social justice, and welcomes the planned redistribution carried out on its behalf by the state.

Differentiation, distinction and selective discrimination are hence essential, but this is not contradictory to the imperative of universalism of benefits (which remains the *sine qua non*): 'In all the main spheres of need, some structure of universalism is an essential prerequisite to selective positive discrimination; it provides a general system of values and a sense of community; socially approved agencies for clients, patients and consumers, and also for the recruitment, training and deployment of staff at all levels; it sees welfare, not as a burden, but as complementary and as an instrument of change.'[39] Universalism is a necessary pre-condition for any policy of planned redistribution. Simply, it is not by itself sufficient to remove formal barriers of economic and social discrimination and combat the heritage of neglect.

The problem today is thus how best to differentiate without stigma within the framework of a universalist welfare structure. The aim must

be to find ways and means 'of positive discrimination without the
infliction, actual or imagined, of a sense of personal failure and
individual fault.'[40] Today, positive selective discrimination must take
place without those who benefit being given any sense of second-class
citizenship, without any hurt being inflicted.

The question is not whether we ought to redistribute social rights,
but of how to do so without stigma. Some will object that this is
impossible: 'How in some respects can we treat equals unequally and
in other respects unequals equally?'[41] Titmuss, however, considered
redistribution without stigma to be both possible and desirable, and
offered the following hints on technique:

Consider first costs. Here Titmuss envisaged graduated and progressive national insurance and health service contributions[42] in place
of the (Beveridge) system of flat-rate contributions, which he dismissed as nothing less than 'regressive poll-taxes'.[43] In general, 'there
is a case for more redistribution through taxing the middle and upper-
middle classes more heavily by making them pay higher contributions
for, e.g. medical care and higher education.'[44] A flat rate means that
the poor pay a higher percentage of their income than the rich in
contributions. A progressive rate would eliminate that abuse and also
permit the burden to be adjusted to individual circumstances (say, by
making allowances for dependents possible in case of need).[45]

At the same time, tax allowances to all and sundry regardless of
need should be suppressed: 'Reduction of tax allowances for children
and old people is by far the simplest, most equitable and least costly
administrative device for preventing "excessive benefits being paid to
those who do not really need them".'[46] Because of the progressive
nature of the income tax system, such allowances represent a greater
subsidy to the rich than to the poor (and may thus represent an
indirect state contribution to the private sector of education and the
'old boy network').

Titmuss believed that in future a greater percentage of the costs of
welfare services should be met out of general taxation. This builds in a
progressive bias and also means that revenue will come from taxes
levied on unearned as well as earned income.[47] Moreover, and this is
largely implicit, he believed too that there should be a general re-
examination of the nature of the tax system. Consideration ought to
be given to the tax-unit (the spender or the earner?), the tax base
(income or wealth?), the balance of taxation (between taxes on income, taxes on outlay, and taxes on capital), and to the problems of
avoidance and alienation. Tax-loopholes ought to be plugged, and

hence Schedule A tax (on the imputed rent that owner-occupiers pay themselves) should be reimposed: its disappearance has been a valuable subsidy to home-owners.[48]

Turning now to the side of benefits, the chief point to note is that Titmuss stressed the importance of impersonal classification. Selective discrimination must mean discrimination between groups as to needs but not between individuals as to incomes: 'There is a case for more selective services and benefits provided, as social rights, on the basis of the *needs* of certain categories, groups and territorial areas (e.g. Plowden's "educational priority areas") and not on the basis of individual *means*.'[49] The aim is, in short, for 'positive discriminatory services to be provided as rights for categories of people and for classes of need in terms of priority social areas and other impersonal classifications.'[50] Such discrimination on a territorial or group basis does not create 'separate, apartheid-like structures'[51] for the dependent, and those who are able to pay are not cut off or excluded. The state services are not left with a purely residual function since, even where resources are concentrated on those groups particularly at risk, there should in no case be the erection of formal discriminatory barriers between the socially superior and the socially inferior. In all cases benefits must remain citizen-based and as-of-right.

To combat dependency, benefits may have to be tailored in such a way as to appeal most of all to the targeted groups in the population. Thus, for example, 'special educational policies directed towards equalizing opportunities for higher education'[52] may be necessary if the children of the underprivileged are to represent a significantly greater percentage of university students. A university could discriminate selectively by admitting (particularly to vocationally oriented courses) older students who do not possess minimum entrance qualifications but compensate for lack of examination performance in secondary school by greater strength of motivation. And as well as opening alternative doors, a university could open a greater variety of doors: it could almost certainly attract more working-class children by offering more 'specialized, vocational career courses',[53] courses which are bound to be more attractive than the humanities to children from poorer homes. Indeed, university admissions policies might even have deliberately to be geared to the general objectives of social planning: 'We may need to develop systems of quotas designed to widen higher educational opportunities; quotas for departments, for faculties and for courses, and quotas for different categories of students. Interestingly, it was only the intervention of the British government during the Second World War that led the medical schools to institute a quota of 10 per cent for the intake of women students to read for medical qualifications. This interference with academic freedom assuredly benefited society as well as women.'[54] Universities, in other words, must 'respond to the welfare objectives of the wider society',[55] even to the extent of sacrificing some of their 'academic freedom'. While each lecturer must remain free to teach as befits his own conscience, the same does not apply to the institution: 'In institutional terms ..... there are and must be limits to freedom,'[56] particularly as the university system, left to itself, does not automatically and optimally satisfy the needs of the community.

It is not just at the university level that there should be reform of the educational system in the cause of planned redistribution of life-chances. Titmuss argued that in Britain, compared with the United States, education was deeply divided by class and privilege; and showed that even in 1961 a very high percentage of bishops, high court judges and bank directors (and, by implication, other élites) were educated in independent schools, especially Eton.[57] From this he drew the following conclusion: 'Until we, as a society, can rid ourselves of the dominating influences of the private sector of education we shall not have the will to embark on an immensely higher standard of provision for all those children whose education now finishes when it has hardly begun.'[58] It would be true to say, however, that the abolition of the public schools is not a topic to which he returned often.

Alongside education, social security is another area in which the principle of selective discrimination can be applied with success. Labour's National Superannuation Bill of 1970, for example, both redistributed income from the rich to the poor and concentrated help on those whose need was greatest:

Firstly, the Bill proposed blanketing-in within a twenty-year period: 'That is to say, instead of having to wait for forty-seven years (for male new entrants at age 18) – the period for which people would have had to contribute in strict actuarial terms – full "dynamised" pensions would be paid within twenty years. This meant that all those currently over the age of 40 would be heavily subsidised – a redistributive effect particularly favouring married women re-entering the labour market and older immigrants from Commonwealth countries.'[59] The young paid for the old, the white for the coloured, and the sacrifice was compulsory.

Secondly, the pensions were not to be minimum or subsistence but adequate, so as to guarantee a reasonable standard of living to old people not in possession of occupational welfare benefits or private insurance without their having to undergo the indignity of applying for means-tested Supplementary Benefits. The definition of subsistence, moreover, was to be dynamized (i.e. continually redefined in relation to rising standards of living). Here again we witness the overthrow of the actuarial principle of equity, that each individual should and can pay only the costs of his own pension. The scheme 'thus presumed a willingness by society to accept an enlarged role for collective altruism in the future.'[60]

Thirdly, contributions were to be earnings-related, not payable at a flat rate. This meant that additional revenue for the scheme could be raised without costing an excessive burden on the low-paid, and also that manual labourers were able to increase their contributions early in life when they reached their peak lifetime earnings (unlike white-collar workers, whose peak occurs just before retirement). Again, benefits as well as contributions were to be wage-related, but here only up to a stated maximum. This would ensure a narrowing of the gap in old age between rich and poor: 'Adequacy was defined in terms of a guaranteed income in retirement for an average earner and his wife of between 50 to 65 per cent of their combined pre-retirement life earnings. Because of the effects of the redistributive formula built into the scheme, the low wage-earner would receive a higher proportion.'[61] Titmuss made similar proposals himself in recommending to the Government of Mauritius a skewed system of wage-related superannuation benefits in which the relationship between contributions and benefits was not to be the same for all levels of (past) income: 'The scheme should be designed to aid the lower-paid worker more than the higher paid. We recommend, therefore, that the lower-paid workers should be treated more generously than other contributors and should receive rather more than they would be entitled to on a strict actuarial basis. Taking account of need in this way is one of the major distinguishing differences between social and private insurance.'[62]

Fourthly, there was to be redistribution in favour of a number of classes of women. The policy of blanketing-in meant that women would not lose pension rights through late entry into the labour-force (nor through absence from work due to child-bearing and child-rearing, sickness, unemployment, or periods of retraining). Moreover, not only were dynamized benefits to be credited to women in virtue of interruptions in their own careers, but they were also to acquire firmer rights over their husband's payments: 'For example, a woman divorced before the age of 60 will have a legal right to take over her ex-husband's dynamised contribution and credits record for the period both before as well as during the marriage. Widows aged 50 or over will have the right to inherit the husband's full personal rate of earnings-related pension.'[63] Thus, the new scheme was 'a new charter for women, whatever their civil status. Social security, especially in its longer-term aspects, is predominantly a problem of women and the prevention of poverty among women.'[64] Titmuss also believed, however, that unnecessary positive discrimination should be rooted out, and that this was the case with the present practice whereby women, who have a longer life expectancy than men, nonetheless retire younger. Clearly, 'there is no justification here for a lower pensionable age for women.'[65]

Education and pensions are eminently suitable terrain for selective discrimination. So is insurance against disease and mishap. Titmuss advised the Mauritians to introduce a system of national insurance with wage-related contributions and flat-rate benefits. The latter were to be at a rate of 30 Rupees per month. There was, however, to be an important exception based on demonstrated and certified medical need: 'The standard rate of benefit which we recommend is as close to the general level of wages as seems safe. There are, however, certain cases of sickness – for example, tuberculosis and deficiency diseases – where a high level of nutrition is essential to recovery. When such cases are diagnosed by medical officers we would like to see a higher level of benefit paid (Rs. 45 a month). This higher level of benefit would depend upon the specific recommendation of a Government medical officer and would be subject to review by the insurance medical officer. In such cases, considerations of the incentive to work are much less relevant and are anyway secondary to the need to restore working capacity.'[66]

Medical need is obviously an important justification for positive discrimination in favour of a group. Thus in Mauritius, where anaemia, malnutrition and undernourishment are all common among young children, Titmuss felt that free milk should be provided for all pre-school children and where possible a nourishing school meal for older ones.[67] And he welcomed the fact that blood for transfusion is in Britain made available to haemophiliacs regardless of the ability to pay.

In summary then, we see that there are a number of ways in which a society can skew the distribution of welfare towards those in greatest need and thus discriminate selectively within a basically universalist structure of benefits. Understandably, we need to note 'the importance of the connections between, for instance, bad housing and inability to profit from education,'[68] and to remember that our attack on dependency must be made on several fronts at once. We are simply deluding ourselves 'if we think that we can equalize the social distribution of life chances by expanding educational opportunities while millions of children live in slums without baths, decent lavatories, leisure facilities, room to explore and the space to dream.'[69] And we need to think big. Titmuss believed, for example, that there should be redistribution between nations as well as within nations, and looked beyond the welfare state to a welfare world. Such a world, he was pleased to report, is well on the way to becoming reality. After all, 'inequalities between nations are now being considered in much the same way as inequalities within nations and between social groups.'[70] Here once again, *what is* is rapidly becoming *what ought to be*.

The process, however, is not automatic, and it was here that Titmuss distanced himself from the models of Radcliffe-Brown (who sought to prove 'that the organic nature of society is a fact')[71] and Talcott Parsons (who attempted to sustain an 'equilibrium-order concept'[72] which is mechanistic, conservative and self-stabilizing). In such models integration and adaptation result spontaneously, with the implication that government intervention in the process of social equilibration is both unnecessary and undesirable. In Titmuss' model, on the other hand, the self-stabilizing order need not be the optimal order; and universalist public provision in the field of welfare is likely to be necessary to combat stigma, ensure the provision of social benefits to cover social costs, promote integration and involvement, and create an infrastructure that allows for planned redistribution of life-chances and for differentiation without stigma.

The counterpart of the models of the Radcliffe-Brown and Talcott Parsons in the economic sphere is the 'metaphysical individualism of the nineteenth century'[73] that was championed by the Victorian economists, who strove 'to establish a competitive, self-regulating total market economy.'[74] Unfortunately, their methodology is unacceptable, since the 'abstractions of economic thought' do not situate the individual in the group and hence ignore the existence of social needs altogether. And, besides that, their conclusions are wrong: the market mechanism not only represents an amoral and a social instrument, but an instrument which in the social welfare field is strikingly inefficient.

The fact is that state provision of universalist welfare services is preferable to the private sector equivalent on purely economic grounds alone. Thus, even if allocation of welfare by the market mechanism were not acceptable for social reasons, state intervention would still be desirable to attain the very goals that the liberal economist himself so much values. The last battle in the war against laissez-faire is evidently to be fought in the enemy's own camp.

The market has failed, and the reasons for this failure compared with state provision may be examined under four headings: quality of provision, choice, quantity and price. We will examine these economic criteria in some detail in Part Four.

10 Part Three: an Evaluation

Universalism is the key concept in Richard Titmuss' unique and important 'Institutional Redistributive Model of Social Policy', which its author describes as follows: 'This model sees social welfare as a major integrated institution in society, providing universalist services outside the market on the principle of need. It is in part based on theories about the multiple effects of social change and the economic system, and in part on the principle of social equality. It is basically a model incorporating systems of redistribution in command-over-resources-through-time.'[1]

In this chapter we shall attempt to evaluate the concept of universalism in the context of the institutional redistributive model, and in particular to demonstrate that Titmuss' arguments are not entirely free of disappointing obfuscations and loose ends. We shall divide our discussion into two sections, the first concerned with the handmaiden function of social welfare and the second with that sense of belonging to a national family which the welfare state is alleged to engender.

(a) The Handmaiden Function

Some of the economic and social costs of production are borne by the individual producer or consumer. The incidence of others, however, falls on the whole community. Titmuss tends to argue that such costs are imposed by the group on itself, and that society has a duty to intervene to prevent them from lying where they fall. He tends to reason that such costs are the price of economic growth, and that the state has no equitable alternative to picking up the pieces. He thus tends to neglect the fact that many social costs are not imposed upon society by itself but on the majority by a minority, on the whole by a part.

Society, in truth, is not at all times a harmoniously functioning organism where each part plays its role in furthering the objectives of the whole. Rather, society may to some extent usefully be seen as a network of particularistic interests. In arguing that social costs should be borne by the collectivity as a whole rather than by those individuals and firms who derive the associated benefit, Titmuss is treating the welfare sector as the mere handmaiden to the interests of the market sector. In assuming that social costs must be borne by the welfare state, he underestimates both the power of science to isolate such guilty parties as there may be and the desirability of doing so. This will become apparent if we look at three examples.

Consider first the individual. It is perhaps salutory to reject the axiom that the improvident poor have brought their ills upon themselves. Titmuss, however, goes to the opposite extreme and appears to neglect altogether the responsibility of the individual for himself and his family. It is conceivable that some ills are not socially but individually generated (the result of, say, voluntary unemployment, excessive gambling, incessant smoking and non-stop drinking, over-indulgence in child-bearing); and that in such cases the responsibility ought to remain in the private sector. Perhaps some costs *ought* to lie where they fall, for a reduction in the present-day importance of individual responsibility could well provoke an increase in the incidence of irresponsibility at some time in the future.

The point is that a residualist sees means-tested benefits as desirable in order to help the poor in the short run until they can take off into self-sustained growth, while Titmuss did not often look beyond relief of present symptoms (partly because of his organicist bias, partly because of his humanitarian wish to be non-judgemental) or wonder if treatment might not prevent eventual cure. If welfare as of right were to result in a reduction in self-help, however, it could easily encourage such socially irresponsible attitudes as a reduced propensity to save, lessened self-reliance, heightened immobility in the labour-market, or diminished parental concern for children. State intervention itself might inhibit vital changes, either intentionally (as where an upset in the traditional way of life is held to be socially undesirable) or unintentionally (as where state services themselves are unadaptable, unresponsive and conservative). And it might lead to abuse. Titmuss admits that it is 'preferable both economically and socially that a man should work for a wage rather than subsist on a dole,'[2] but underestimates the need to prevent malingering where the individual perversely prefers the dole to the wage. Because he ignores abuse, of course, Titmuss is also able to ignore the police-state controls over the life of the dependent that are often necessary, in conditions of scarcity of resources, to prevent waste. Such controls represent a man-made threat to civil liberties and a heavy social cost on the poor.

Clearly, not all social welfare is 'compensation for disservice caused by society',[3] and much does represent a net increment in well-being. The poor, moreover, are by no means the only recipients of this free gift, as the example of education reminds us. The state supplies the vital input of trained manpower through the provision of schooling on a universalist basis, and thereby generates a costless surplus for a few individual beneficiaries. Titmuss was aware of the differential private and personal return that results from differential public investment in human capital,[4] but provides no discussion of the moral implications of a state activity which finances the affluence of the few with the contributions of the many. In the case of education, society benefits, but so (disproportionately) do some of its component units. This disproportionate benefit could naturally be reclaimed by, say, loans rather than grants to students, or a special graduate tax (levied, at the very least, on graduates who acquire a costly education at public expense and then seek their fortunes abroad); but Titmuss, here as elsewhere, was reluctant to see a man pay for his own particular consumption of welfare.

Consider now a second example of the handmaiden function, the case of the firm; and here it is important to realize that private industry receives a long list of complementary inputs from the collectivity. One of these we have already mentioned: industry in the new industrial state receives the important gift of trained manpower (which is likely to augment its profits) and is not to be asked in return for a counter-gift in the form of compulsory on-the-job training or a special levy on education-intensive lines of production. Another, similar free gift is roads: understandably, the car industry and the private motorist are pleased not to be assessed the full cost of this complementary product by means of an economic road-fund levy, and are delighted that much of the burden is shouldered by the general taxpayer (who, statistically speaking, is not a car-owner and does not himself benefit from the car-owning aspect of the 'British way of life'). The justification of public provision of roads in terms of how much 'we' (the community) value cars is, however, a naïve use of the concept of consensus, and also implies a questionable hidden subsidy. After all, if the cost of roads were passed on to the consumer or back to the producer, then possibly fewer cars and fewer roads would be demanded; and if high indirect taxes would prevent the consumer from buying a particular commodity, it is hard to see why the non-consumer should subsidize him in his purchase.

The same line of argumentation applies to health care. In the Titmuss model, the welfare state treats victims of road accidents free of charge, as it does sufferers from bronchial ailments brought on by air pollution or excessive smoking. Such redistribution could be corrected by user-charges, which relate costs to benefits on a selective basis. It is only equitable that motor insurance premiums be mobilized to compel those citizens likely to make above-average demands on society's medical services to pay an above-average share of the costs; and that the smoker be asked to cough up (via an easy-to-collect health service contribution payable on each packet of cigarettes) at least part of the extra burden on society's resources that will result from his choice as a consumer. To Titmuss, nonetheless, even the idea of such charges was taboo.

It is, however, somewhat unfair to expect the community as a whole to subsidize the diseconomies imposed by industry and enterprise, somewhat unjust not to place as much emphasis as possible on the taking of preventive and corrective action by those parties most immediately responsible for diswelfares, social costs and leaks in the fabric. Many readers, moreover, will find Titmuss' passivity in this context infuriating. Thus he is almost certainly right to note that there is no monetary profit in the provision of hostels for coal-miners with chronic bronchitis or of anti-air pollution devices; but he is almost certainly wrong then stoically to deduce that these costs must hence either be borne by the community as a whole or else allowed to lie where they fall. Such a deduction is not only fallacious but it is morally equivalent to arguing that patients suffering from serious illness caused by the presence of dangerous substances in foodstuffs must be treated free of charge in public hospitals because there is simply no financial gain to cake-makers from employing less noxious types of food-dye. The point is that the cake-makers could be compelled by law not to impose burdens on the community from which they alone derive the benefit; and that, since the law already in fact intervenes to defend the consumer against the producer, there is no reason why it should not similarly be enlisted to defend the interests of the employee against the employer. Firms could, for example, be counselled to take out third-party insurance to protect workers in dangerous trades (rather than relying on the national family to finance the above-average burden on welfare facilities) and employers could be required themselves to cover the costs of maternity-leave and crèches for the offspring of mothers in their employ; while agricultural workers living in tied accommodation, rather than facing the possibility of being turfed out of house and home and driven on to the parish when their masters find it no longer possible to squeeze an economic return from them, might be guaranteed security of domicile until the day they die. Employers will gnash their teeth; but, after all, fringe benefits are not unknown in industry, and what Titmuss neglects is their institutionalization as a desirable and equitable alternative to social welfare.

As a third example of the handmaiden function, let us consider the case of social solidarity. Titmuss notes that 'the welfare state has evolved as a particular manifestation of Western democratic societies'[5] and that all now have such welfare systems. He also notes, however, that social welfare is 'a major force in denying the prediction that capitalism would collapse into anarchy'.[6] A cynic might argue that this means in practice tension-management and a system where welfare professionals have the function of helping the 'deviant' (Christ as well as the cat-burglar) to fit into an insane society. A cynic might argue further that if society produces the dependent, then it should cease doing so rather than attempt to resocialize its victims within the framework of the *status quo*. A cynic might even argue that individual therapy can actually impede necessary social changes, particularly insofar as it in the last analysis represses real social tensions that ought perhaps to come out into the open in the interests of genuine social equilibrium.

An instance of this unexpected latent function of the welfare state is to be found in the case of crime. Titmuss argues that, for children who leave school early and live in deprived conditions in an urban slum, 'crime is 'the one remaining major form of acquisitive social mobility',[7] and demonstrates an admirable tolerance of such deviants (who, after all, cannot in his view be held fully responsible for the character society has stamped on them in the course of economic upheavals lasting four generations or more). Deviation, Titmuss argues, is 'a social ill or a "social problem"'[8] and reminds us that the devil in the piece has 'more of the character of Bentham than of Freud'[9] (which in strict logic should perhaps mean compensation of the criminal for bearing the costs of other people's progress). He recommends selective discrimination as a means of reclaiming the most alienated for what is basically a going concern, and thus as a handmaiden to the existing economic and social system. Yet it is precisely here that his model is beset with difficulties. Should society have, for example, no unique value consensus, then whose values are to be inculcated in the deviant? And might not healthy as well as unhealthy deviance be repressed (no one knows whether a new line of academic research will be 'socially relevant' until it is explored; or, again, many reformers such as Tawney appear intellectually deviant until the central value system catches up with them)? In any case, the use of the welfare state to curb anti-social behaviour patterns might well be inadequate. The sources of crime, after all, are not purely to be found in deprivation and inequality of opportunity; and may even have something to do with the ethos of the market sector itself insofar as it assigns a superior value to ends than it does to norms. It is conceptually possible that in a society where the central value system rates success above craftsmanship the origins of crime must be traced back not simply to the underdog but further still, to the overbitch.

Another instance of the way in which Titmuss felt the welfare state could repress social tensions is the case of alienation. Titmuss complains about the 'degradation of the worker' in a system of scientific management and advanced technology where 'the machine tends to regulate and control the work'[10]; and notes the contradiction that the manual labourer is expected to be passive at work (the tool of others) and active at home (the master of his destiny and that of his family). Such a state of things leads him to the following conclusion: 'In so far, then, as modern industrial techniques lead to feelings of personal dissatisfaction, to a dispossession of personality, the problem thus becomes a family and community problem.'[11]

What is striking here is that the cure has little or nothing to do with the disease. Titmuss is simply arguing that the pressures of economic growth and industrialization generate tensions too great to be dealt with by the family alone (despite the central role that it plays in all societies) and that this imperative necessitates social involvement: 'It is in this context that we need to see the social services in a variety of stabilizing, preventive, and protective roles. Interpreted in this way, and not as the modern equivalent of Bismarckian benevolence, the social services become an ally – not an enemy – of industrial and technological progress!'[12]

The social services, in other words, are expected to deal with pathological cases and to deal with them in accordance with society's needs and values. Titmuss, however, has little to say about the roots of pathology, and tends to regard as outside his remit the forces in the market sector that cause men to flee across the border into the welfare sector. He makes little reference to possible causes of alienation to be found in boring and unrewarding work; in powerlessness rather than participation; in class conflict and resentment; in lack of social direction beyond acquisition and the pursuit of happiness. He underestimates the responsibility of the market sector for many of the kinds of diswelfare that must be dealt with in the state sector; and confuses the issue by using 'alienation' in the sense of 'anomie', i.e. a sense of malintegration that can be overcome by closer ties of community and common participation in groups. It may be the case that both alienation and anomie have deep social roots; and that a National Health Service can satisfactorily treat neither the symptoms nor the illness.

In such a situation socialism might result, were it not the case that yet another unexpected latent function of the welfare state appears to be socialism-repression. In Sweden, as Gunnar Myrdal has explained, the result of four decades of Social Democratic rule 'has been large-scale social reforms, but practically no nationalisation of industry, commerce or finance .... Sweden now stands as the one country among the developed nations where business is almost entirely left in private hands, even more so than in the United States with its absolutist faith in private enterprise.'[13] This is an important externality of the welfare state, and one about which Titmuss has nothing to say. Naturally, association is no proof of causation. Were it true, however, that the welfare state, by papering over the cracks and concealing the ugly face of market capitalism, also discourages the nationalization of industry and finance, then the discovery would lend some credence to the view of those socialists who argue that the welfare state is not an expression of social integration but of social malintegration, and who explain its origins with reference to the needs of the economic system as perceived by a ruling class; to the existence of class conflict and the need to frustrate socialization of private property; and to the desire of vested interests within the nation to foster a fiction of social integration totally irrelevant in the material circumstances of the times (a case of value manipulation that if accepted would seem to put Titmuss in a very sinister light indeed).

Titmuss did not adequately explore the handmaiden function of the welfare state, as we have seen by looking at three examples (the individual, the firm, and the social matrix as a whole); and part of the reason was his failure to distinguish between social causation and social responsibility.

It is tautologous to say that social phenomena are social facts in the sense that they are observed in a social context. Thus higher fertility rates and earlier marriages (both social facts) indubitably mean shortage of housing and schools (necessitating a social cost); while education, by reducing the rate of illiteracy, increases national efficiency with respect to the use of scarce resources (implying a social benefit). Again, free medical care, by improving the average health of the nation, means that the population is becoming increasingly elderly and hence increasingly more likely to represent a burden on health services. Indeed, the demand for medical care itself is social as well as physiological in origin, and reflects 'particular forms of society and cultural patterns'[14]: 'The more that a society as a whole values success in life and fears death the higher may be its demand for medical care in some form or other.'[15] Even the sensation of pain or stress is refracted through our perception of pain or stress, which may be largely cultural and sensitive to social role-playing. Nowadays, 'more people have grasped the idea that pain can be avoided,'[16] and there is also 'a heightened awareness of what medicine has to offer'.[17] Attitudes to health, disease and the doctor are unambiguously social facts.

Social causality does not, however, necessarily imply social responsibility, and to argue as if it did is functionalism run wild: because each part of the social machine is related to all parts of the social machine, it does not follow that each part is responsible for all parts. Such functionalism masks microsociological lines of causation and conceals the specific allocation of costs and benefits.

In some cases, of course, social diswelfares do necessitate social services. This is the case, for example, with preventive medicine to control infectious diseases. Here the argument for third-party provision is precisely that a third party is involved – not just the consumer (the patient) and the supplier (the doctor) but the whole society as well. A similar argument applies in wartime in the case of neurotic conditions engendered by bombing and air-raids (since such conditions, if not treated, would be a threat to public morale); of orderly evacuation (a desirable alternative to panic flight); of homelessness and injuries caused by enemy action (where in the absence of redress workers would not remain in the cities); and of provision of nurseries for children under the age of five (which release mothers for factory-work and improve the morale of fathers in the trenches). War is a phenomenon which affects every member of the collectivity; and moreover, the government alone in wartime can adequately represent society as a whole when it comes to correcting abuses imposed on some for the good of all.

It is not clear, however, that social diswelfares in *all* cases necessitate social services. Large families impose a burden on schools, but it is not axiomatic that the family is less responsible (less burdened with a moral obligation to pay) than the country within which it lives. And the fact that people know of new antidepressants being manufactured by drug companies does not necessarily imply that the general taxpayer ought to finance the consumption of these drugs by households (whereas he would not finance an evening out for them at the circus). Or in the case of an illegitimate child, because a pregnancy can have individual as well as social causes it need not in itself demonstrate the case for authentic social responsibility. And again, an undernourished child may receive relief from governmental sources and still not represent a diswelfare imposed by society upon itself. The child undeniably exists in a social situation, but the cause of his distress might still not be your fault and mine but that of his parents (who might refuse to take their responsibilities seriously). One could, of course, argue that the parents themselves are the product of their society; but the individual can nonetheless only be made to disappear from the equation by a degree of environmental determinism that Titmuss would not in any circumstances have accepted.

Part of the confusion surrounding the handmaiden function of the welfare state arises because, in trying to be non-judgemental, Titmuss threw out the baby with the bathwater by neglecting the need for a theory of social pathology. Titmuss is at the best of times not strong on causality (witness the inadequate explanations he provides of the growth and integrative functions of the welfare services); and he does not in particular identify the poor in detail or make differential recommendations relative to different causes of an identical state of dependency. Clearly, however, the poor fall into a number of different categories. They might be old-age pensioners without private insurance (but we are not told why they are not insured, and if they are not in part responsible for their own condition through lack of foresight). Or they might be the low-paid (where public relief of poverty possibly conceals the class structure and conceivably obviates the need for minimum wage laws). Or, of course, they might be the redundant who, because they have obsolete skills, bear the costs of technological progress on behalf of the collectivity as a whole. Here we have three separate cases of poverty, all of them social facts and yet each displaying a different percentage of social fault. Relief of distress is naturally laudable in all cases; but where the argument is in terms of charity rather than sociology, the distinction must be made clear.

As will by now have become apparent, Titmuss' theory of the handmaiden function of the welfare state is beset with a basic contradiction. On the one hand social welfare is defined as a system of unilateral transfers, of free gifts to strangers. On the other hand, however, it is also to be conceived of as a way of reimbursing actors for disservices and diswelfares borne in the social interest in the course of progress, and in this latter case reciprocity is implicit: society *owes* the victim a gift in exchange for the gift he has already made to the collectivity (even though the initial gift was compulsory, not voluntary, and despite the fact that there is no way of measuring gift-equivalence with exactitude). Such transfers are not unilateral but represent a utilitarian *quid pro quo*, which indeed may be the handmaiden to economic growth in the private sector as well. This is most notably the case with the provision of essential services complementary to growth in the market sector but not provided by it. In the case of education and health (if not pensions) compassion may well raise national efficiency and productivity; and, more generally, where integration and fellowship replace alienation and crime, even the most sceptical must confess that altruism, in certain circumstances, can be *good business*.

(b) The Sense of Belonging

Richard Titmuss believed that one of the chief active functions of the welfare state is to foster perceptions of Gemeinschaft, common situation and that social solidarity which is based not on exchange of equivalents but awareness of resemblance. He simultaneously chose to neglect the potential breakdown of fellowship under the bracing cold shower of market competition, possessive individualism and economic self-interest. Yet the fact is that in a stratified and commodity-oriented world, an awareness of resemblance (a sense of citizenship and community) is unlikely to develop in the market sector; and that it is many times more unlikely that the welfare sector can really bring into being a social fact that goes so strikingly against the dominant value orientation of the times.

The central problem is that Titmuss' model is a two-sector one, with private enterprise in one box and welfareism in the other; and the triumph of the latter over the former is by no means assured in view of the fact that Titmuss presents no adequate theory of social causality. We are told, for example, that in Britain the gift relationship is strong; while both in America (where the market sector is more extended) and in the Soviet Union (where the market sector is more contracted) attachment to social groups, as measured by the index of voluntary blood donation, is weak. We are not, however, told why. Clearly, the social force that fosters altruism and represses egoism is not to be sought in the economic basis (and perhaps this is why Titmuss seldom mentions private enterprise capitalism by name or calls for its outright socialization): Russia has nationalized the means of production, distribution and exchange, while in Britain and America they remain largely in the hands of private businessmen. But neither can 'the demand for one society'[18] be traced back to the welfare environment, for Russia, like Britain, provides free schooling and a national health service. That crucial variable which promotes a sense of belonging remains, in short, shrouded in obscurity.

Many will in any case be dubious about the validity of philosophical generalizations built around such a flimsy index as the gift of blood. Blood donation is, after all, not a real or permanent unilateral transfer, since the body quickly replenishes the loss. The only cost to the donor is time and discomfort, both modest in comparison with the amount of self-felicitation which follows the gift (and which is itself a form of counter-gift). Moreover, even if Titmuss' 1967 sample survey represents a random sample of the British blood donorship in that year, it is unlikely to represent a random sample of the population as a whole; and hence tells us no more of the social attitudes of the vast majority who do not give blood than a fragment of Socrates' toe-nail would tell us of Socrates. Should the blood donors not share wider social values, it would be a serious methodological error to confound their pathological behaviour patterns with the normalcy of the central value system, or to mistake their altruism for a widespread social fact. Finally, although Titmuss makes much of man's 'biological need to help'[19], he does not say how he knows that nature is on the side of socialism (rather than the 'survival of the fittest' ethos of the market sector); or explain why, if nature in truth is fundamentally so beneficient, it became so perverted as to necessitate correction through the countervailing power of the welfare sector.

The gift of one's life-blood has a dramatic sound. A more meaningful indicator of social responsibility and integration would, however, be the alienation of something which does not renew itself quite so quickly. Statistics on charitable contributions might be a reasonable measure, since the gift of money in actual fact represents a bigger sacrifice than the gift of blood (even if admittedly not quite as intimate); and other significant indices of caring might include unpaid

participation in community self-help schemes, voluntary staffing of
adventure playgrounds and citizens' advice bureaux, the willingness of
workers to cover the tasks of weaker colleagues who might otherwise
be dismissed, the willingness of employers to take on released prisoners
and rehabilitated derelicts out of a sense of social obligation and
'conscience without shame.'[20] Indicators of social irresponsibility and
malintegration are, as it happens, no less easy to find; and here the list
embraces baby-battering, litter on Clapham Common, senseless van-
dalism, strikes of electricity workers in cold weather (imposing the
high cost of hypothermia on the old and the poor), or the propensity
of many solid citizens to offer themselves free gifts at their place of
work, at the local supermarket, and even on public transport (the last
instance particularly naughty since, as Titmuss put it, 'people who
defraud the Government defraud themselves'[21]). A sample survey of
3813 juvenile delinquents on the scrounge would give a very different
picture of egoism and altruism in modern Britain from that which
emerges in the Titmuss study of 3813 blood donors; and the only
legitimate way to decide if we as a national family more resemble the
delinquents or the donors is by recourse to comprehensive macrosociological indicators such as national data on the incidence of crime,
mental disturbance or suicide (the latter being the subject of
Durkheim's model demonstration of how to employ middle-range
functionalism to explore the general through the medium of the
specific). Only by painting on a larger canvas (if, indeed at all, since
the contents of men's minds are notoriously difficult to discover) can it
be determined whether or not British people living in a welfare state
do or do not have a sense of belonging.

A man is rightly to be judged by the sample he keeps; and the fact
that Titmuss opted for the donors rather than the delinquents is truly
a sensitive psychological indicator of his generally optimistic state of
mind concerning the degree of integration in British society. Part of
his attraction is indeed to be explained in terms of what we demand as
well as of what he supplies; for few readers will find totally repugnant
the idea of an Avalon of national unity in which citizens sup on the
milk of human kindness. Equally, however, few readers will find
totally convincing his claims for the vitally instrumental role of the
welfare state in bringing about desired social change. People cannot be
integrated into a community which to them is non-existent; and in the
two-sector model with which Titmuss confronts us the narrowness of
exchanging might well frustrate the social benefits that are attributed
to unilaterality and giving. We shall explore this possibility by looking

in more detail at three services provided within the framework of the welfare state.

First, the National Health Service. The hospital can integrate boss and worker in the same ward and offer them equal access to treatment. It cannot, however, ensure permanent brotherhood and friendship (acting thereby as 'an expression and reinforcement of national unity'[22]) for the simple reason that it then releases its charges when well and restores them to the world of disintegrative differentials in pay, power, prestige, security and facilities. Boss and worker will hardly retain their friendly feeling of a common condition when they resume their acrimonious battle over relative shares in the process of collective bargaining. Here there is a fundamental contradiction between a man's market value and his value as a citizen, since a set of differentials arises in the first case but not in the second. These differentials are determined by a class identity and class conflict, and the variable of social class is thus likely to be an obstacle to integration difficult to surmount by means of adjacent beds in a community hospital.

Second, education. The schoolteacher may treat all children equally and yet still fail to instil a lasting perception of equality: after all, in a dual society the market outside the school will ultimately grade and class his products (not least according to their efficiency in performing the very operations he has taught them). Differentials rather than equality are the market sector's definition of social justice, and this leaves little room for the school-teacher's notions of fairness. As Marris and Rein put it, 'The schools cannot care equally for the education of every child, whatever his skills, unless the man he will become is equally valued, whatever he can contribute. And this no competitive economy can itself ensure.'[23]

Equality of opportunity need not mean equality of outcome or income, and may be an architect of inequality and malintegration in its own right. This is certainly the case with education where, as Titmuss himself reminds us, scarcity of resources limits access to the most valuable forms of training and necessitates rationing by intellect: 'The principle of universality cannot be applied to higher education in any country of the world in this century.'[24] Credentialism, as Titmuss saw, is rampant, but no antidote is proposed to protect those sound and hard-working citizens whose contribution is manual rather than mental from the scorn of their more intelligent former neighbours.

Free comprehensive schooling provided on a universalist basis may clearly have an unexpected latent dysfunction. The meritocrat attend-

ing a school which aims to integrate as well as to educate him may find
that his level of education becomes such that he can in consequence
command a substantial salary differential from an employer accustomed to setting a superior price on a superior input. This superiority
may in turn either reinforce the meritocrat's existing social position or
elevate him to a higher social group; but it is bound inevitably also to
produce social division by distancing him from (not integrating him
with) the boys and girls with whom he was once at school.

Third, income maintenance. Titmuss' propensity to focus on benefits
in kind rather than benefits in cash at least in the context of discussions
on the sense of belonging) obscures the fact that much of welfare
outside the world of the personal social services is divisive rather
than integrative and actually promotes inequalities. Titmuss, moreover, showed an extraordinary blind spot in welcoming the Labour
Party's National Superannuation Bill, which would have carried
the market valuation of the low-paid beyond retirement age
through its earnings-related benefits and would have (alongside the
fact that the low-paid are less likely to receive occupational pensions
than the well-to-do) contributed to the perpetuation of 'two nations in
old age'[25] that he was so anxious to terminate.

The point is that any earnings-related cash benefit tends to carry the
market conception of social justice over into the welfare sector; and
yet that many wealthy families simply could not manage on an
averaged flat-rate payment unrelated to what they are accustomed to
earning and spending. A redundant executive out of work will suffer
acute loss of self-respect if his family's living standards fall too far
below what they and the members of his reference group are used
(conspicuously or inconspicuously) to consuming; but differential
provision nonetheless does imply buying a First Class ticket for a first-
class gentleman and a second class ticket for a fifth-class lout. Such
inequality, such compartmentalization, is the inevitable consequence
of any policy of income maintenance save one which focuses uniquely
on the squalor and misery of absolute deprivation.

Absolute deprivation remains a problem, and the very poor are still
with us. Titmuss believed, however, that in an affluent society the bulk
of distress would become relative rather than absolute in nature: 'In
retrospect, we see now that the centre of concern in 1911 was with
states of absolute poverty: today, we are more concerned with relativities
– with states of relative injustice; conditions of relative need; questions
of relative choice and opportunity.'[26] It is unfortunately not self-
evident that, in a demi-market economy, altruism will be triumphing

over egoism to such an extent that some tax-payers will be willing to finance others, who are not paupers but obese and may already have a car, a television and a potting shed. A taxpayer who cannot afford a house of his own may begrudge the taxes he pays to finance a council flat for someone else; and Titmuss (convinced as he was that social policy reflects 'the expressed wish of all the people to assist the survival of some people'[27]) neglected the danger that the cost of integrating Jill might be alienating Jack. In absolute terms, the 'deprived' (relatively speaking) might be quite well off, and 'injustice' in the sense of 'inequality' might not be enough in a parliamentary democracy to generate any real eagerness to cover the costs of caring. Titmuss is exaggerating the sense of belonging now to be found in a demi-market economy if he believes that a businessman will be enthusiastic to make sacrifices in order that his competitor may be treated for a nervous breakdown; he is forgetting that when it comes to the needs of those popularly stigmatized as deviant (say, the unmarried black mother of six with a drink and drugs problem) the average citizen may well be less non-judgemental than the social worker in evaluating potential dependents who demand more from society without supplying more in return; and he is neglecting the important fact that the balance in the political market and on polling day might be swayed against collective responsibility by the existence of a hungry tax-octopus whose tentacles embrace progressively more and more citizens in its constraints of freedom.

Part Four

THE FAILURE OF THE MARKET

11 The Failure of the Market I: Quality

The quality of provision in state welfare systems is superior to that in private welfare systems, as can be seen from three examples relating to health services: the quality of blood available for transfusion, the quality of professional attention received from medical personnel, and the quality of care offered by the general practitioner.

Consider first the quality of blood. In America in 1965–7 about one-half of blood collected (including blood obtained through plasma-pheresis programmes) was purchased, and a further 40% tied by blood-insurance or blood-replacement contracts.[1] This indicates, as we have seen in Chapter Seven, a low level of involvement in the community (especially since voluntary donorship in America is on the decrease, while at the same time there is evidence of an upward trend in the percentage of blood supplied by paid donors).

Statistics are deficient, but it appears that the paid blood donorship is not a typical or representative cross-section of the community. A large percentage of paid donors appear to be poor, unemployed, unskilled, black and male, substantial numbers of them Skid Row denizens, drug addicts and others who live by selling their blood (at $5 to $25 a pint) to commercial blood-banks and eventually to the rich, who can afford to write cheques for blood.[2]

Unfortunately, these mercenary donors are often bled more frequently than accepted international standards recommend, thereby risking iron deficiency anaemia (such 'ooze-for-booze' donors probably having an inadequate diet in any case). Moreover, the risk of transmission of hepatitis via contaminated blood is probably six to ten times greater if the donors are paid suppliers than if they are volunteers.[3] Titmuss quotes evidence which suggests that in America hepatitis hits one in 25 to 50 patients receiving a transfusion, with death occurring in up to 20% of these cases. Even if the fatality rate is lower, it is nonetheless high: 'There may be 75,000 cases of hepatitis yearly, with almost 10,000 deaths.'[4] And the number of cases is increasing. Clearly, commercial markets for blood mean a high risk to the patient of disease, disability and death, resulting from contamination.

Contamination is intimately linked to conflict of interest. A potential donor, recognizing that a full medical history might disqualify him from giving blood and thus deprive him of money, is likely to conceal a history of hepatitis, malaria, syphilis, drug addiction (possibly using unsterilized and infected needles) or alcoholism, and to understate how often he has already been bled. Anyone who is willing to walk in and sell his blood in order to buy food, drink or drugs cannot be completely trustworthy; and yet whether the gift of blood is beneficial or harmful to the recipient depends on the truthfulness of the donor and his willingness to provide rather than withhold information. In such a case, 'one man's untruthfulness can reduce another man's welfare.'[5] In America, where blood is reduced to the level of a consumer good, the commercial donor has a positive incentive not to tell the truth about himself and his circumstances: 'Because he desires money and is not seeking in this particular act to affirm a sense of belonging he thinks primarily of his own freedom; he separates his freedom from other people's freedoms.'[6] The social costs of such irresponsible untruthfulness are plain to see: 'The dishonesty of donors can result in the death of strangers.'[7] Moreover, even private blood-banks do not adequately screen donors lest they themselves lose money; and deliberate negligence or calculated carelessness as to the health of donors is only a step away from illegal forms of dishonesty (such as the use of insanitary equipment, or the mislabelling and updating of blood). Profit-motivated commercial blood-banks may actually seek out Skid Row donors (despite the obvious health hazards involved): such donors, after all, charge less for their blood than a higher class of donor would have done, and every good businessman has the sense to buy in the cheapest market.

The ignorance of the recipient as to whether blood is infected denies his consumer sovereignty. The patient must trust the doctor who must trust the donor, since often the laboratory cannot identify diseased blood until it has been transfused into the recipient (who is thus the guinea pig used to test its quality in conditions of medical uncertainty). Such trust is likely to be misplaced. In America, the consumer has less freedom to choose healthy blood than in Britain, and he must pay more for his transfusion. In America, 'he pays a far higher price for a more hazardous service.'[8] The destruction of a system of unilateral transfers in a world of competitive capitalism may well mean the destruction of the patient's life.

In Britain, on the other hand, blood is of good quality. In view of the potentially lethal nature of human blood and the risk of disease transmission, rigorous standards are maintained in the selection of donors. Health histories are ascertained to ensure that the donor is a healthy specimen. Again, the donor himself is likely to be truthful since there is no financial incentive to be otherwise: all British donors are volunteers making a free gift, as against only about 7% of blood suppliers in the United States.[9] Moreover, the system of large-pool plasma is avoided. It has commercial advantages in that such plasma is easier to store and transport than small-pool plasma, but there is also a greater risk of transmission of infection;[10] and as a result plasma in Britain has for some time been prepared from small pools of blood drawn from fewer than ten donors.[11]

British arrangements maximize honesty and ensure that blood will be safe and pure precisely *because* it is not an economic good or part of a commercial transaction. In Britain there is little or no risk of infection through hepatitis following a blood transfusion,[12] and the reason is that the values of the economic market-place are not applied to the world of social welfare. In Britain, in other words, 'freedom from disability is inseparable from altruism.'[13]

The British system benefits the donor as well as the recipient. In Britain the donor is not bled more than twice a year (although he could safely be bled more often in an emergency), and thus his freedom is preserved: there is no risk of iron deficiency anaemia brought on by over-bleeding. This danger is greatest for the poor and the underfed, who ought not to give blood in the first place but may in a commercial system be attracted to do so by the promise of cash. A commercial system is hence 'potentially more dangerous to the health of donors'[14] than a public system of free gifts, which protects the donor against himself.

Consider now a second example of inferiority in quality of provision that exists in the private sector, namely inferior standards of professional practice on the part of medical personnel. The reason here once again is conflict of interest, and specifically the threat to the doctor's professional ethic that might arise in a market system.

To begin with, let us note the existence of this ethic: 'In all Western societies it is declared that the supreme object of medicine is service and not personal profit. The essence of professional behaviour and the patients' confidence in a profession is thus *predictable service to people.*

Predictable, in this context, can be translated as 'truthful'. Practitioners have a fiduciary trust to maintain certain standards predictable to patients.'[15]

Yet, in a market system where the doctor sees himself as a small businessman or entrepreneur selling his services to the highest bidder in the same way that another tradesman sells tomatoes or beetroot, he may find himself confronted with the temptation to be less than truthful. Because there cannot be consumer sovereignty in a market where the patient is inadequately educated in medical science to make a valid choice, the patient must have confidence in his doctor; and there is evidence that the doctor has often abused that trust for personal profit. A doctor who has invested in a hospital or pharmacy[16] or who has staff privileges at a particular clinic such that he gets a percentage of the fee paid by each patient he recommends is likely to be tempted to prescribe unnecessary treatment.

In a free market economy buyer and seller are presumed to be on an equal footing. In the case of medicine, however, because of non-shared knowledge and information, the patient is unambiguously subordinate to the doctor and has no alternative but to trust to the expertise of the specialist. The patient must accept that the doctor knows best and be prepared to sacrifice his freedom of choice to his respect for higher authority. The danger is that the doctor will abuse the confidence the patient has in him. After all, the fact that the potential demand for medical care is unknown causes consumers, unable to plan ahead, to purchase insurance, and such pre-payment may tempt untrustworthy doctors to perform unnecessary operations: 'Their inability to make choices leads some consumers to demand "their rights" written in partial prepayment contracts – X number of days in hospital, access to an expensive drug, three X-rays a year and so on. Similarly, some doctors put up their charges when they learn that consumers have already "bought" particular units of service. A rise in the price of an appendectomy – which has been "bought" but which may or may not be necessary – will cost the consumer nothing in the short run or until the policy comes round for renewal.'[17] Such 'imbalances and distortions ..... must inevitably flourish in market situations in which science has increased the relative ignorance and sense of helplessness among consumers.'[18] Witness, for instance, the situation in Mauritius, where the patient is often at the mercy of an unscrupulous pharmacist. There, 'the pharmacist who is asked to prescribe at the counter is inevitably tempted to try and dispose not of the customer's disease but of his own expensive and unwisely purchased stock.'[19]

Medical care is not a personal consumption good, a commodity like any other, precisely because the consumer is almost completely ignorant of the need for or quality of a particular service and cannot in any sense be said to 'shop around'. He cannot know *whether* he needs surgery to have his appendix or tonsils removed, or estimate *how well* the operation was performed. Nor can he usually benefit from evaluation of experience: the typical operation is a once-for-all affair, and the patient can only judge treatment once he has had it.

Such ignorance makes the doctor-patient relationship an unequal one; and the realm of inequality is expanding due to the scientific revolution. New drugs, new techniques, new instruments, new degrees of medical specialization all represent not greater freedom of consumer choice but an enlargement of the realm of the patient's ignorance: 'It is now impossible to explain medicine to a sick man, for it is as difficult to describe Hodgkin's disease or acute leukaemia in everyday language as it is to find everyday words for a curve of the fifth-degree or the notion of entropy.'[20] Naturally, the problem of understanding is even greater for the mentally retarded and the mentally ill, for the educationally deprived, or for the new immigrant with a different value system. Yet these consumers too have a right to good medical care.

The market cannot satisfactorily provide what the consumer cannot reasonably value; and price competition in medicine is hence not a viable proposition. By subjecting doctors to the law of the marketplace, a society distorts doctor-patient relationships, lowers standards of professional practice, and fosters feelings of cynicism, frustration and dissatisfaction among clients. In America, indices of the palpable breakdown in relationships and standards are the following:

First, there is information from attitude studies and surveys. For example: 'A nationwide study commissioned by the American Medical Association in 1958 reported that 44 per cent of all the people interviewed had had "unfavourable experiences" with doctors, 32 per cent of them so unsatisfactory that they said they would not return to the same doctor.'[21]

Second, there is an increasing resort to self-medication. In the absence of the defence 'deriving from a relationship with a personal, generalized doctor the patient in the United States has increasingly to resort to self-diagnosis.'[22] Witness too in this context 'the growth of various forms of medico-scientific charlatanism, resort to the corner drugstore, chiropractors, naturopaths.'[23] Consumer sovereignty in such a situation may come to mean surrender to the makers and advertisers of drugs (and to the media, who grow fat on such advertising), although, of course, 'in another sense, it is the patient who has surrendered by worshipping uncritically at the shrine of science.'[24]

Third, malpractice suits abound in the United States. It was estimated in 1969 that 'one in five of all physicians in the United States had been or was being sued for malpractice.'[25] The situation was particularly bad in Southern California, where 'physicians in practice for five years faced in 1969 a 50-50 likelihood of being hit with a claim and the attendant threat of a lawsuit.'[26] Yet such suits 'are thought to be a symptom of a breakdown in doctor-patient relationships;'[27] and the rising incidence of such claims may hence be taken as testifying to the existence of consumer dissatisfaction with American medicine. Suits have been filed if the patient had simply not been fully informed of every possible side-effect that could arise from an operation (and explanation is no easy task when one is talking to a sick non-specialist who needs surgery without delay), or if a miracle drug did not work; and the point is being reached where there will even be a suit if the patient does not fully recover or dies.

Malpractice suits necessitate malpractice insurance, the cost of which is high and rising. In California, to take the most extreme example, 'the young doctor has now to pay around $820 a year for such insurance.'[28] And even worse than the cost of cover is the danger of being without: a doctor unable to obtain insurance at all may be faced with bankruptcy, and in any case feels his career and clinical freedom to be restricted.

Moreover, the patient does not take out what the doctor pays in: 'Commercial insurance cover against malpractice cost physicians approximately $75,000,000 in 1968 but of this sum awards to patients totalled only about $18,000,000. The difference went on sales and promotion, administration, profits and legal fees.'[29] Neither doctor nor patient really benefits from such a set-up; and hence, in order to eliminate the middleman, compulsory arbitration is often agreed upon before commencement of treatment. Yet in this case the patient signs away his right to sue the doctor in the event of malpractice, and must also face the contingency of potential negligence at the very start of the doctor-patient relationship. Such a system is unlikely to breed an atmosphere of trust.

Titmuss believed it was imperative, in the light of the above evidence on the failure of the market mechanism when applied to medicine, to resolve the conflict between the doctor's professional ethic and his economic self-interest: 'In the social situation in which the doctor finds himself today, I happen to believe that the conflict between professional ethics and economic man should be reduced as far as is humanly possible.'[30] This can only be done by taking medicine into the state sector: 'I regard the National Health Service Act as one of the most unsordid and civilized actions in the history of health and welfare policy. It put firmly doctors on a footing with university teachers, and patients on a footing with university students. Both professional groups – of doctors and teachers – are expect to give generously of what they know without a premium being put on time or knowledge. The presumption in the relationship is thus more social than economic.'[31]

In Britain, unlike the United States, there is no conflict of economic interest, and the doctor can be true to his ethic of disinterested service. This does not, of course, mean that he is expected to be indifferent to monetary compensation, only that his salary comes to him irrespective of work performed so that he in practice spends his time performing a series of unilateral transfers.

Titmuss was fully aware of the role monetary incentives could play in the welfare state. He pointed out, for example, that 'to attract, recruit and staff the social services ..... raises competitive issues of pay, rewards and career earnings,'[32] and reminded the reader that higher taxes to finance higher welfare spending could thus reflect higher input-prices rather than increased quantity of product supplied. Again, he noted that Supplementary Benefits staff are low-paid relative to the earnings of bank and insurance clerks, with the understandable result that 'for years these offices have been understaffed while banks have often been over-staffed.'[33] He is here speaking of administrators. Elsewhere, however, he attributed the same sensitivity to pecuniary incentives to medical professionals themselves. Thus he advised the Mauritians that the geographical spread of doctors in a co-ordinated national health scheme owes something to the fact that doctors respond to differential capitation fees by moving into under-doctored areas: 'Experience in other countries has shown that it is very difficult to induce doctors to live outside the main urban centres ..... We hope to solve this problem in Mauritius by the incentive method which is used in Sweden. We believe that doctors will be attracted to live in less popular areas by the offer of a free house and some monetary differential.'[34] On the other hand, however, he seems to have believed that the Tanganyikans should adopt standardized national salary scales. Since he also argued that vacancies in Tanganyika should be filled by advertising, not compulsory posting, it would appear likely that unpopular posts would not be filled at all. Titmuss was aware of this danger: 'We accept that such a system could result in the least attractive candidates getting the least attractive appointments and, occasionally, in vacancies going unfilled for some period.'[35] Yet the report still makes no mention of differential monetary incentives.

Whether a local scale or a national scale is applied, the principle remains the same: professionals' pay in the state welfare system should be independent of results, just as academics should not be paid according to students' marks in final examinations. Only then will doctors be free to exercise their professional curiosity and to pursue the supreme ethic of service rather than the mundane aim of profit. Such disinterested service is the guarantee of predictability, quality, and high standards of workmanship. The patient can with more justification put his trust in a salaried professional than in a small businessman or tradesman paid by piece-work; and such trust is an important part of personal freedom. In Britain there is no breakdown of confidence in doctors: there were only 264 cases of alleged professional negligence in 1967,[36] and the subscription for malpractice insurance in 1969 (the same year as the cost in California was $820) was only £6.[37] Moreover, appeal mechanisms are organized by the Service itself, so that recourse to expensive litigation becomes unnecessary. The greatest protection for the consumer is not the right to appeal, however, but the knowledge that the doctor can be relied upon to give truthful information.

Doctor as well as patient benefits from state medicine. In Britain, the doctor is freed from the dilemma of how to treat people reluctant to seek proper treatment because they cannot pay. Due to the existence of the National Health Service, cost is no obstacle to care and the doctor does not have to ask himself if the patient can afford the optimal course (say, a specialist consultant, a drug, a spell in hospital, an expensive surgical aid, or a series of X-rays). Such a system means enlarged professional freedom for the doctor, who becomes able to treat the patient according to medical rather than monetary criteria.

Moreover, the doctor in Britain has security of tenure, and can also count on a guaranteed income. He is thereby freed from financial worries such as how to compete with his rivals, or whether or not he will be able to attract enough customers into his shop without sacrificing his standards to the whims of the sovereign consumer. In a system of private medicine, on the other hand, practitioners are often forced by their patients into prescribing 'useless and sometimes dangerous'[38] medication: after all, in a competitive situation, withholding drugs might cause the doctor to lose clients. Such was the situation in Tanganyika at the time of Titmuss' visit: 'The people of Tanganyika now broadly accept the efficacy of Western medicine in its curative aspects. Indeed, there is a danger of too much reliance being placed on the drug and the injection. There is a growing tendency for patients to "shop around" among various doctors and agencies in the urban areas in the belief that any and every ill will be cured if a powerful enough drug is obtained.'[39] Clearly the conjunction of modern medicine with the market mechanism is an explosive one: 'It must be difficult, in these days of scientific drugs, to take money from patients and give nothing tangible in return.'[40] Yet such patient pressures may represent an unhealthy and wasteful substitution of the curative for the preventive, and thus an incorrect attitude to the problem of disease. In Tanganyika, 'as a result of the success of modern methods of treatment of yaws and certain other diseases, health has come to be regarded as a matter of being injected when sick rather than adopting radical changes in diet and personal habits;'[41] and a private practitioner who refused to supply wonder drugs would soon find himself bereft of clients and fees. His British counterpart is much more fortunate.

As a third and final example of the way in which the quality of provision in state welfare systems is superior to that in private welfare systems, let us note the fact that the community in Britain benefits from a symbiotic relationship with the professional. The key here in the medical field is the existence of a flourishing network of general practitioners.

The scientific revolution has meant that medicine has become increasingly complex and increasingly subdivided into fields of specialization. In America, the general practitioner is rapidly losing ground to the specialist; and such family doctors as remain are likely to avoid personal involvements and 'time-consuming human relationships.'[42] This is deplorable: 'More and more people may be losing an essential patient liberty – the advice, protection and defence which the general practitioner is in a position to give his patient.'[43] Fortunately, in Britain, in contrast to the United States, the general practitioner still has a role to play. His functions in the British system of social medicine are four in number:

First, the family doctor is a bridge between the patient and the specialist and hence a valuable safeguard against the jargon of science. He is a vital defence against narrowmindedness, standing as he does between his patient and 'the excesses of specialized technocracy'[44]: 'This role of standing between the patient, the hospital and over-specialization increases in importance as scientific medicine becomes more complex, more functionally divided and potentially more lethal. These developments are enlarging the need for the detached, non-specialist diagnostician – the doctor who can interpret scientific medicine and the process of diagnosis and treatment to the patient according to the circumstances of each case, and without any functional or financial commitment to a specialized area of practice.'[45] Like any other generalist, the general practitioner has a wide range of knowledge; and he is thus an informed counsellor to whom the patient-consumer can turn for advice.

Second, the family doctor knows the patient as a person and not simply an envelope of symptoms to be passed from one anonymous expert to another while all along too ill to be able to make personal contact with any of these learned strangers. The family doctor is a family friend who has known the whole person in health as well as in adversity; and, knowing the patient in his own home and environment, is less likely than an outsider to mistake the symptoms for the disease. Moreover, and perhaps most important of all, the family doctor values communication with his patient, a quality too often absent in the chilly departmentalism of modern in-patient treatment: 'The demands that people make on society are greater when they are ill than when they are well. Yet the advent of science has made it more difficult, in social and psychological terms, for the hospital as part of society to meet these demands. More science means more division of labour and more experts – more of the mysteries of blood counts, X-rays, test-meals, investigations, case history taking and so forth. These, in turn, mean more departmentalism and, all too often, more departmental thinking. As A. N. Whitehead warned us, the fixed person for the fixed duties in a fixed situation is a social menace. He is particularly a menace to the sick person who is in more need, rather than less, for explanation and understanding.'[46] Evidently hospitals have not always grasped that 'courtesy and sociability have a therapeutic value,' as the following example of the 'discourtesies of silence' in one British hospital illustrates: 'Drugs were given without inquiry or explanation; examinations were made in silence; infra-red lamps were set going without explanation; people left hospital without explanation. The barrier of silence seemed impenetrable.'[47] Patients were simply not told anything.

Third, the existence of the general practitioner ensures that medicine will be community medicine. The general practitioner is a member of the local community and is, via his own integration, in a position to ascertain local needs. He thus helps to increase the potential participation of the hard-to-reach, who neither articulate their problems nor ask for help (and whose participation increases pressure on scarce resources without increasing revenue to finance services, a welfare-objective far from the world of profit-maximization). Universalism in social policy must refer to the take-up of benefits as well as to the elimination of any means test; and because even in the era of the National Health Service medical care is free on demand only to those who request it (who are aware in the first place that they have a need and a right to treatment), the hard-to-reach must be contacted, helped to make choices between alternatives, guided round a complex world of welfare. Only in this way can the welfare state become *de facto* comprehensive. Clearly, the family doctor plays a vital role in this process, a role which is strengthened where he links up with other local welfare workers as part of a team.[48] This is already happening in Britain, where nowadays 'society is moving toward a symbiosis which sees the physician, the teacher and the social worker as social service professionals with common objectives.'[49] Via the co-ordination that only really exists in a system of state provision, the physician becomes part of a community care network that also provides rehabilitation and training centres for the physically handicapped, short-term stays in hospital for examination or treatment, services for the mentally ill, the unmarried mother, the disturbed child, the materially deprived, the aged. The key words here are collaboration, co-operation, co-ordination, communication, consultation, continuity of care, and such integration of services cannot but mean better treatment: 'The accepted purpose of the health service is to treat the individual who has some malfunction in such manner as to restore him to health, and that must involve the individual's mental, emotional and social functions as well as his physical functions.'[50]

Fourth, community medicine benefits not only doctor and patient but also society as a whole. Some of these benefits are primarily sociological in nature: we have, for example, already noted the socially integrative effect of treating all patients alike rather than arranging them in a descending scale going from those best able to pay (and therefore most deserving) to those least able to pay (and therefore least worthwhile 'in genetic or productive terms'[51]). But some of the benefits are clearly economic, even if non-commercial. This is the case with preventive medicine. To the hard-to-reach patient himself, 'blindness prevented is an enlargement of freedom.'[52] To society as a whole, however, it is no less a source of freedom, since it circumvents later pressure on resources: 'Humanitarianism can ..... lead to substantial financial savings; insofar as blindness can be prevented, economic resources may be saved on a large scale for many years if old people are helped to go on living in their own homes without the need for institutional care and other services.'[53] The same benefit arises from the control of infectious diseases in a society. Again, the general practitioner can, by helping to set 'standards of behaviour'[54] for other local professionals, raise the efficiency of the community care network; and he can, by rationing medical resources according to need rather than means, contribute to the maintenance in good repair of the labour-force. Naturally, the benefits that arise from general practice are difficult to measure with precision 'in the language of productivity or the economic market place.'[55] Yet inability to quantify should not be allowed to blind us to the real benefits that arise in a medical system which allows for more home visits and community care, and makes the doctor a family friend rather than an impersonal business-man.

The general practitioner, then, has four valuable functions to perform in the British system of social medicine. Unfortunately, however, he suffers from stigmatization and self-stigmatization brought on by the fact that he is less technically expert than the specialist, the scientist or the consultant in a big hospital. Nowadays, there is growing esteem for the specialist in all walks of life, while 'the generalist is too detached and indeterminate to be in favour in a world of professionalism and expertise'[56]: 'Because those who specialize (who aim to fulfill a restricted determinate function) have a higher status in our society the general practitioner becomes more conscious of inferior status. He is the indeterminate man; the one who is more uncertain of his place in the scheme of things; who is uneasy because he has to spread himself so widely and has no special role to perfect; no special skill by which he may himself achieve higher status in his profession.'[57] The general practitioner is aware of his diminished status and simultaneously has a sense of other-directedness brought on by the belief that his authority has been undermined by the experts and the march of science. He must, however, be helped to overcome his anxieties and insecurities through an increased awareness of the crucial role he plays in society. And, paradoxically, time as well as socialism is on his side. Scientific progress means more than just specialization. It also means that the general practitioner can now treat more diseases (in the home and the community) that would previously have been lost to the impersonality of the hospitals. Science, by giving the family doctor a new lease of life, thus plays its part in keeping the standard of social medicine high.

12 The Failure of the Market II: Choice

Freedom of choice is essential to man's self-respect and Titmuss himself rated it highly: 'As an individual ..... I would like to be sure that when my time comes my right to be eccentric in old age will not be eroded by busy, bureaucratic planners. I shall want some rights to some choice of services; not a simple confrontation between, on the one hand, institutional inertia, and, on the other, domiciliary inaction.'[1] The welfare state is justifiable precisely in terms of the need to defend the freedom of consumer choice.

It is, of course, true that 'people cannot "shop around" for social work support, medical care, education and cash assistance (at least in Britain) to the same extent as they can for shoes or cabbages in the private market.'[2] The consumer can, however, nonetheless successfully press for a meaningful range of choices: 'Choices may be offered, for example, within social security programmes as to alternative ways of calculating and paying social security benefits as of right. Choices may also be offered between benefits in cash and benefits in kind; for example, old people living alone or unmarried mothers on low subsistence standards and in poor housing conditions might prefer the security of residential accommodation to higher assistance payments. Choices may also be offered within services in kind; for example, the alternatives of medical care and welfare services for disabled people in their own homes or in institutions or a combination of both through the provision of day hospitals, night hospitals, home-for-the-weekend hospitals, day and night homemaker services, occupational centres, and so on.'[3] And as for pensions, the state could offer 'options and choices as to the form in which certain benefits are paid; for example, mortgage advances at retirement age, earlier payment of retirement pensions in special circumstances, etc.'[4]

The state sector is more likely to provide a range of options and choices in response to consumer pressure than is the private sector. The reason is that, whereas nowadays both sectors are highly bureaucratized, bureaucracy in the former sector is socially accountable while in the latter sector it is not. Two examples will serve to demonstrate the superior sensitivity of decision-taking in the welfare sector. The first example refers to insurance; the second concerns medical care.

Consider first the case of insurance. In Britain, Titmuss argued, we know little or nothing about how private insurance companies and pension funds actually exercise their power, despite the fact that as investors they dominate the City and are the single greatest source of new capital. They are secretive and publish few statistics on current market values of their assets and hidden reserves. Nor do they reveal the precise goals of the handful of managers who exercise powers of decision-making on behalf of the mass of shareholders and policy-holders. Here we have a clear illustration of economic and social power 'concentrated in relatively few hands, working at the apex of a handful of giant bureaucracies, technically supported by a group of professional experts, and accountable, in practice, to virtually no one.'[5] It is power that is centralized and yet power without responsibility; and the community has no guarantee that this power is being used to satisfy social welfare objectives rather than the personal and private priorities of secretive and faceless bureaucrats in large corporations.

The community is not consulted about the employment of the funds at the disposal of huge institutional investors and has no alternative but to accept the choices made by corporate officials on behalf of the collectivity. Yet this leads to an unbalanced allocation of social resources, since the portfolios of corporate investors are skewed. Insurance companies do not invest in the slums of Lancashire or in the dying coalfields of South Wales and Scotland but in profitable undertakings such as office blocks and luxury flats in London. Such choices sacrifice both the welfare needs of society and the quality of the environment, and are made with an eye to private profit and organizational aggrandisement rather than social growth. These choices are made without consumer or social participation by men who are themselves hardly a representative sample of the population: 'Of 126 directors of 10 leading British companies in 1956, one-half went to Eton and six other public schools; most of them belong to a small circle of clubs among which the Carlton is the most popular; a high proportion are titled; and most have extensive connections with industry, finance and commerce.'[6]

Moreover, in the private insurance market individual liberty is ignored: 'There is no appeal machinery in this costly and bureaucratic system; no opportunity to speak up as there is in the National Insurance system.'[7] The private system is totalitarian, lacks democratic participation, and offers few if any channels for the redress of wrongs. Yet wrongs abound. There may be lack of consultation (as where the scheme is not voluntary but compulsory and the employee insured cannot choose to contract out and spend his earnings in some other way), lack of alternatives on offer (as where there is little choice of cover, insurer, or between, say, earnings-related and flat-rate schemes), lack of full transferability of rights on change of job (an obstacle to mobility and thus to economic growth in an increasingly fluid economy), lack of survivor's rights on the death of the policy-holder (a loss of accumulated savings and cause of much hardship to the widow left behind). In any case, redress of grievances is only possible if people know their rights, and since there are in Britain no less than 65,000 different occupational pension schemes (each with its own rules and structure of benefits) it is no surprise that the consumer is often too confused or too ignorant to make meaningful decisions: 'Millions of those who are members or ex-members of such schemes know little about their rights, benefits and expectations.'[8] Thus even if there were a formal appeals mechanism in the private insurance market, consumers would not necessarily have recourse to it.

Many abuses in the world of private pensions and insurance have been brought about by the twin economic factors of oligopoly and economies of large scale. Mergers and amalgamations have reduced the number of firms in the industry, and it is a characteristic of markets dominated by a small number of large participants that price competition tends to wither away. Simultaneously, giant organizations have sought to reduce administrative costs by substituting group risk-rating for individual risk-rating and calculating premiums on a simple cost-plus basis. Hence 'prices and policies have become more standardized over larger areas of group insurance; less subject to risk- and experience-rating; possibly more subject to power-rating.'[9] The decline in the practice (if not the fiction) of individual risk-rating unfortunately leaves many difficult cases without any cover at all (or may at least force them to pay higher prices) simply because they do not lend themselves to standardization. Here 'equity suffers in the conflict with bigness and those who suffer most are those who fail to fit neatly into pre-determined large-scale classes, categories and groups.'[10] This is bound to harden 'felt discrimination'[11] and the sense of stigmatization.

Unexpected and inequitable redistribution may arise within a scheme once a system of individual risk-rating (where individual premium is tailored to individual risk) is replaced by group risk-rating (where premiums and risks are pooled on the basis of broad categories such as age, sex or occupation). Blanket cover is discriminatory insofar as it means that good risks pay for bad ones, and hence those who are classified in a system based on standardization may have as legitimate a complaint as those who are excluded. The absence of individual risk- and experience-rating means 'that the true social costs are not borne by the dangerous industries and causative agents' and that 'the "bad risks" are not charged the true market price. The poor in non-dangerous trades may thus be subsidizing higher income groups employed in other trades. The poor, safe driver may be subsidizing the rich, bad driver.'[12] Again, the decline of medical examinations for life insurance means that the healthy pay for the unhealthy;[13] and also that a healthy man in a statistically unhealthy occupational or racial group may be overcharged in flagrant disregard of considerations of equity. In any case, 'actuarial risk- and experience-rating in group insurance is today far from being an exact science.'[14]

Much regressive redistribution from the poor to the rich shelters under the pretence of equality of treatment. Suppose, for example, that pension benefits for all policy-holders are related to final earnings. This nominal equality conceals a serious injustice, since such earnings are maxima for highly-paid non-manual occupations but not for low-paid manual workers whose earnings may peak early in life. The practice of relating pensions to earnings in, say, the last three to five years at work thus 'discriminates against manual workers whose higher earnings in earlier years are not reflected in their pension benefits.'[15] Besides that, social change means that the low-paid in practice have a higher labour-turnover, and hence a higher propensity to lose all or part of their welfare expectations (i.e. their deferred pay, taken in the form of insurance and pensions cover). Benefits lost are then shared out among those who remain in their jobs or enjoy 100% transferability. In this way 'many private pensions schemes, which include manual and non-manual workers, tend to redistribute claims on resources from lower-paid to higher-paid employees.'[16] Furthermore, in calculating pension benefits average mortality tables are applied. Yet the rich have on retirement a longer life-expectancy than the poor and hence tend to draw out proportionately more in benefits where premiums are the same: 'The poor pay more in the private pension market because they are poor and are statistically treated as non-poor.'[17]

In summary, then, it is Titmuss' opinion that choices in the private market for insurance are made by a small number of executives in a small number of organizations, and that these choices are demonstrably neither in the social nor the consumer interest.

The situation in the state sector is quite different. There social security reflects the social interest, since publicly provided services are directly accountable to the collectivity and its elected representatives. Since nowadays, whether in the state or the private sector, insurance is provided not in the competitive markets of the elementary economics textbook buy by huge bureaucracies, it is all the more urgent to substitute accountable political authority for the insensitivities of naked economic and social power.

Faith in politicians and the public bureaucracy means the ability to plan (with the implication that reprivatization signifies not just a flight from government but a 'retreat into irresponsibility'[18]). It means the ability to discuss, since more information is available about social than about private insurance. Finally, faith in politicians and the public bureaucracy means that social security can serve consciously chosen social goals.

Naturally, 'as the "social" role of insurance has become more powerful the area of conflict with actuarial principles has widened.'[19] But, after all, the private sector too has moved away from the principle of individual equity, away from the idea of taking out what you put in. Some redistribution is going to occur in either case, and the state should simply ensure that choices as to who gains and who loses represent social rather than minority interests. Many social choices, moreover, cannot be made by the consumer even in the most flexible of markets. The use of social security to encourage married women to return to work, to compensate the redundant, or to narrow the gap between rich and poor in retirement implies a set of choices which can only be made by the collectivity as a whole.

Let us consider now a second example of the superior sensitivity of the state sector, namely the case of socialized medical care. It is important to remember that medicine is in the last analysis a social science and must 'change in sensitive association with the changing needs of society'.[20] Hence its administration and the structure of services provided must be planned but adaptable and, in the interests of democracy, unquestionably subject to social control. A market system is unable to assure this social control: the consumer's ignorance means he is unable to make intelligent choices and, besides, he is unable alone to make choices which involve the collective rather than purely the individual interest.

Titmuss believed that social policies are irresponsible where they are 'imposed without democratic discussion' and 'without consideration of the moral consequences which may result from them'.[21] In Britain, fortunately, responsible rather than irresponsible social policies in the medical care field appear to be the order of the day, and result from the interaction of four groups of actors:

First, there are the consumers. In the National Health Service, the public is able to reveal its preferences; and consumer participation already has some successes to its credit in influencing choices made. Thus public opinion outside the hospitals has, for example, brought about improvements in the food served to patients and in the arrangements made for parents to visit sick children.[22]

The complex administrative structure of the National Health Service has in the past clearly not inhibited criticism based on examination of the facts and on expression of public expectations. The quality of treatment in the Service has notably been raised by the presence in it of the vocal middle classes: 'Their continuing participation, and their more articulate demands for improvements, have been an important factor in a general rise in standards of service – particularly in hospital care.'[23] Integration combined with active consumer pressure has in the past undoubtedly meant a levelling upwards of standards; and in the future consumers are likely to be even more demanding because of *embourgeoisement*. Society may thus expect improvements in the quality of its health services to result from 'the rising standard of expectations of medical care from a more articulate, health-conscious society'.[24] Indeed, the spread of education and of 'middle-class attitudes and patterns of behaviour'[25] has already meant that there is 'a tendency for more people to adopt a questioning and critical attitude to medical care'.[26] One social fact leads to another: 'As standards of education and living rise greater significance is attached to sensations of pain as signals of danger to the individual and his sense of self-preservation.'[27]

A better-educated population will be increasingly less subservient and disciplined, increasingly more demanding of improvements in the quality and quantity of medical services. Such popular criticism will be healthy for doctors as it stimulates professional self-examination: 'For too long, university teachers outside Oxbridge, family doctors outside Harley Street, workers in other professions, and bureaucrats in Whitehall and Town Hall have lacked the challenge and incentive of a critical clientele. In this setting of unequal relationships, low standards have flourished. In the long run, an educated public opinion is, as J.H.F. Brotherston has said, the most powerful ally of the medical profession.'[28]

Politicians and administrators must be made aware of the options that the consumer would like to have, and thus the state sector should be sensitized even more to the demands of the public. This could be done through the 'institution of consumer advisory groups and the development of local committees and tribunals to hear complaints, to redress wrongs and to criticize administrative agencies.'[29] It is, of course, precisely this opportunity to advise on the nature of his preference-patterns that the consumer so much misses in the private sector.

With the aim of consultation in mind, Titmuss recommended in Tanganyika that an Area Hospital Advisory Committee should be set up in each region: 'The regional medical officer or his deputy would take the chair and the members might include the area medical officer, one or more representatives of the local authority, and a representative of the local community development agency. All meetings of the committee would be attended by the medical superintendent, the chief nursing officer and the administrative assistant. We do not envisage such committees meeting frequently (perhaps once every three months) but we regard such a committee as a valuable means of co-ordinating the area health service, quite apart from providing local democratic representatives with opportunities to participate in the responsibilities of hospital management.'[30]

In view of Titmuss' conviction that decision-makers should follow as well as lead the consumer, these recommendations are surprisingly modest. One notes, for example, that the committees are to consist chiefly of professionals and that not consumers but officials are to be represented (a proposal which has corporatist overtones). One notes too that the committees are to meet rarely and to have no more than advisory powers. Of course, demand-led change is difficult to implement in a country where the bulk of the population is uneducated. Yet it is striking that in his work on the British National Health Service, Titmuss hardly mentions consumer participation via committees and councils at all, and appears to be extremely dubious of the efficacy of such outside interference. His view seems to have been that there is no substitute for a technical, administrative or professional background if one is to find one's way round the complexities of the modern hospital system: 'I do not wish to join with those who would make a mystique of administration, but I must say that in my experience most lay members, newly-appointed, of a hospital board or management committee are pretty useless during their first year of office.... It is not until perhaps half the three years have gone by that a new member can play a really useful part in hospital government.'[31]

Whatever his views on direct consumer participation, however, Titmuss unquestionably believed that the consumer interest should be taken into account wherever possible, and that institutional arrangements should be such as to ensure considerable consumer freedom. Such freedom obtains in the National Health Service. In Britain the patient is free to have a private as well as a National Health doctor; to choose his doctor and change him; to select between treatment at home by his family doctor and treatment in hospital. The consumer has the freedom to seek treatment he could not otherwise have afforded (a valuable benefit to a poor man whom the private sector is likely to reject because his needs are excessive relative to his economic power) or might have had to postpone (possibly until a need for preventive is superseded by a need for curative medicine). The absence of a money nexus between doctor and patient heightens cordiality and gives the patient the security of knowing proper treatment will be provided regardless of how much (or how little) it costs. Again, the integration of medical care in a comprehensive welfare state means the removal of other uncertainties related to medical care. Thus, for example, since society provides not just hospitals but income maintenance in convalescence to its members, it permits the ill to enjoy the luxury of not returning to work too soon after treatment. Such a luxury is an important part of the freedom of consumer choice.

Second, there is the press and the other mass media. Titmuss believed they had a valuable role to play in disseminating information about the social services and in providing informed criticism of their operation. He also believed, however, that the mass media were not properly fulfilling these functions because of their generally hostile attitude to the welfare state, coupled with a tendency to trivialize great issues into simplified black-and-white matters. These shortcomings of the media were due in turn to their obsession with audience-ratings (since these influence the sales of publications and the promotion prospects of journalists) and to their fear that support for government as against private enterprise would lead to a loss of advertising revenue.

Naturally, Titmuss does not propose nationalization of the media. Indeed, he makes no direct recommendations at all on how to convert the media to the service of society, and only very indirectly hints at the need for controls of some sort: 'Just as academic freedom can justify anything (what Tawney once called "creating a darkness and calling it research"), and clinical freedom justifies private practice and profit-making hospitals in the USA, so the freedom of the press can justify mass entertainment, the commercialisation of sex and the commercialisation of privacy. As these unlimited freedoms become more pervasive, society – and particularly at this point in history American society – becomes harder and harder to govern. It is not widely known that during the first six months of 1971 more people were murdered in New York alone than all the American soldiers killed in Vietnam during the same six months.'[32]

Despite his deliberate evasiveness on how exactly to discipline the press, Titmuss clearly had a pronounced authoritarian streak, as one would expect from an interventionist with a belief in monolithic bureaucratized government. It is certainly tempting to wonder if he would have countenanced censorship of Milton Friedman and Herbert Marcuse, two authors whose work shares a common 'critique of authority – and particularly authority in the shape of government'[33] and who are both in part to blame for the movement towards reprivatization of welfare services. It is unlikely that Titmuss would ever have advocated such censorship. It is, however, possible that he would in his heart of hearts not have found it totally repulsive.

Third, there are the medical professionals: 'In the modern world, the professions are increasingly becoming the arbiters of our welfare fate; they are the key-holders to equality of outcome; they help to determine the pattern of redistribution in social policy.'[34] The reason for this development is a technical one: a society does not choose to rely on the experts, it is forced to do so, since they alone can maintain quality control in an era of specialization and scientific revolution.

The expert *does* know better than the mass of the people (which means that in both private and public sectors decision-making by professionals takes the place of simple consumer sovereignty). The problem is that he may also be insensitive. Professionals do have greater power than ever before. The task now must be for society to make them 'assume greater social responsibilities to match their added knowledge and the power that accompanies it.'[35]

Unfortunately, professionals are often resistant to social change because of their own vested interests, because of professional inertia, or because of a fear that acceptance of criticism from without will diminish their prestige and influence and circumscribe their ability to control their own affairs. Professional groups may, for example, irresponsibly obstruct the re-allocation of economic resources according to social priorities by refusing to participate in drafting reforms and by rejecting the suggestions of outsiders: 'Criticism from without of professional conduct and standards of work tends to be increasingly resented the more highly these groups are organized.... As the social services become more complex, more specialized and subject to a finer division of labour they become less intelligible to the lay councillor or public representative. A possible consequence is that, collectively, more power may come to reside in the hands of these interests. The question that needs to be asked of professional associations is whether they are prepared to assume greater social responsibilities to match their added knowledge and the power that accompanies it. Professional associations are not the only repositories of knowledge, but they are the repositories of a very special kind of knowledge; and the establishment of proper relations between them and the democratic State is, today, one of the urgent problems affecting the future of the social services.'[36]

Besides their status insecurities, professionals may be unprepared to act in the social interest because of the blinkers imposed by their class background: 'In Britain and other countries, the professionals are largely recruited from the middle classes; professional workers come from homes and educational institutions where they have little contact with manual workers and people from different cultures. Thus, they bring to their work middle-class values in the processes of giving or withholding medical care, education, legal aid and welfare benefits. The model of the ideal pupil, student, patient and client is one with middle-class values and a middle-class tongue. This process, subtle and often unconscious, partly explains why in Britain, under universally available welfare services, the middle classes tend to receive better services and more opportunities for advancement. This is understandable; we all prefer the co-operative patient or client; motivated to achievement, anxious to learn, anxious to work.'[37]

Finally, professionals may be out of touch with the social interest because of excessive specialization, departmentalization and hierarchization of services. There is a danger that 'separate interests, divided skills and special loyalties', by provoking 'an increasing fragmentation in responsibility for the treatment of the individual patient', may lead to a shift in emphasis 'from the person to some aspect of his disease'[38] and to an 'absence of critical self-examination arising within the hospital'.[39]

Against these negative forces must be set, however, the continued presence in the British health service of generalists as well as specialists, and also the sense of organic solidarity that results from interdependence among professionals and leads to demands for the social planning of medical services: 'Scientific advances have profoundly influenced the social and administrative organization of medical care. This is true of both "private" and "public" forms of organization. Conversely, the ways in which medical services have been organized have influenced the application of science in medical practice. One effect of the interaction of these forces has been to make the doctor more dependent on the natural sciences for the practice of his art and, consequently, more dependent on society and his fellow doctors for the provision of an organized arrangement of social resources now recognized as essential for the application of modern medicine.'[40] Here we have a clear case of the division of labour operating with a self-transcending mechanism to promote in the last analysis greater co-operation, teamwork and pooling of effort (and less fragmentation of skills) than would otherwise have been the case. Science may pull the health services in opposite directions, but the resultant of the stresses is clearly in the direction of collective effort.

Social planning must be complemented by education for citizenship so as to train the doctor to treat the patient as well as the disease. The sociology of the patient must no longer be neglected: 'The problem of the quality of medical care is in part an administrative problem; in part a problem of human relations in the hospital; in part a problem of bringing the hospital as a social institution back into society where it properly belongs and from which it has for too long been isolated. Today, all those who work in the hospital need to care much more about how and why the patient comes; what the person experiences as a patient, and what happens to the patient when he returns, as a person, to society.'[41]

Such education should be both general and specific. On the general level, doctors should be trained to see medicine as a social science and not to lose sight of the fact that they are dealing with human beings as well as symptoms. On a more specific level, professionals should be trained to make socially useful choices: there is no excuse, for example, for being so blinded by one's own class bias that one forgets to ensure that the low-paid get an adequate share of high-cost health facilities.

Fourth, there are the politicians and the civil servants. They are accountable to the public and thus make decisions with an eye on the value consensus. They emphasize considerations of social rather than individual utility. And they ensure co-ordination, integration and balanced development on a national scale: 'Only by planning can scarce administrative and professional staff be used to the best advantage.'[42] Planning means co-operation, liaison, and the avoidance of wasteful duplication, but it 'does not mean uniformity in every respect'.[43] In Tanganyika, where Titmuss and his colleagues recommended an integrated health service responsible to central rather than local government, they took care to note that they did not mean 'the centralization of every decision. On the contrary, we would urge the need for devolution of responsibility within an overall plan as this is essential for flexibility.'[44]

The option of choosing a planned, co-ordinated and socially responsible health service is an important aspect of freedom of choice. After all, medicine is a community problem: 'The traditional division between curative measures which benefited the individual and preventive measures which protected the community as a whole is becoming less distinct, if not obsolete.'[45] Much that benefits the individual also benefits the community. Much that benefits the community also benefits the individual.

13   The Failure of the Market III: Quantity

The quantity of welfare services available to the consumer in a system of free enterprise is deficient when compared with the situation prevailing in a welfare state. There are in America, despite the prevalence of the market, a number of shortages and bottlenecks in the sphere of social policy, as will be apparent if we take three examples from the world of medical care:

First, there is a growing shortage of doctors and nurses in America (as indeed of social workers, town planners and teachers), a shortage which has had to be met in part by tapping supplies of foreign-trained professionals. America in this way saves the cost of training, but it also robs poorer countries (particularly unfortunate where the doctors come from the Third World) and provides evidence of bad manpower planning. Titmuss' argument loses some of its force, however, when he confesses that Britain too (despite her planned and co-ordinated welfare state) is in the same position and is also a net recipient of human skills (a form of foreign aid) from the Third World.

Second, and possibly a more conclusive piece of evidence, there is the case of hospital beds. In America, despite the 'advent of more profit-making hospitals as a source of capital gains',[1] the market-mechanism evidently fails to stimulate adequate supply: 'The number of hospital beds per 1,000 population dropped from 9.7 in 1948 to 9.2 in 1962. In England and Wales over the same period the number of staffed beds rose from 10.2 to 10.3.'[2]

Shortages are worse when one disaggregates. In terms of services, for example, at the same time as there was over-building of small, in-efficient but lucrative private hospitals in the United States, 'the shortage of less expensive long-term facilities – for example, mental hospital beds – grew worse.'[3] Profit-orientated private hospitals are re-luctant to provide services which, however valuable socially, are nonetheless money-losers: 'The corporations who operate these hospitals have decided not to treat "indigent" or "charity" patients and not to provide emergency, obstetrics or paediatric departments.'[4] And in terms of geographical availability of care, 'there has been little change over the past twenty years in the striking disparities in the state ratios of physicians to population in America.'[5] There thus appears (despite the alleged existence of the fabled natural corrective forces of the market) to have been a lack of balance in American medical services: 'There is serious over-building of hospitals and gross duplication of expensive equipment in some areas, growing shortages in others, and a general trend towards greater maldistribution in important sectors of medical care.'[6] Lack of co-ordination and planning means it is sometimes impossible in America to get a bed in one hospital while a number of beds are empty in another. This is quite apart from the socially fundamental divergence between services in the suburbs and services in the ghettos: even in the suburbs there can be delays to see the doctor and hurried consultations.[7]

Local shortages and a maldistribution of services are endemic to a health system based on the principles of free enterprise. In Britain before the Second World War, for example, there was a seriously uneven distribution of medical skill relative to social needs: 'A few areas of the country and a small section of the people were abundantly served with medical and nursing skills, but in many places, especially the economically depressed areas, there were widespread shortages.'[8] Consultants and specialists tended to concentrate in London, and even within London doctors tended to settle in wealthier areas. Before 1939, there were 'proportionately seven times as many general practitioners in Kensington as in South Shields.'[9]

Since 1948, however, the situation in Britain has radically changed: '"Unnatural" or governmental forces have undoubtedly brought about an improvement in the geographical distribution of doctors and medical resources in Britain since 1948.'[10] In Britain, the introduction of the National Health Service has removed the financial incentive to the general practitioner of operating in a well-to-do area. It has encouraged equality of access through planning of services. And it has reduced structural imbalances and local shortages to the minimum via co-ordination (in place of the anarchy that results from a private system of independent and competitive units).

The intricate proposals for a co-ordinated three-tier health service that Titmuss and his colleagues made to the Government of Tanganyika demonstrate just how much scope there can be for a system of integrated medical services. The Report called for 'the creation of a chain of centres which will bring together curative and preventive services',[11] and recommended that, in order to spread the health-care network reasonably evenly through the population, the country be divided into 40 'health areas'. Each area was to consist of twenty-five health clinics, five health centres, and (except in remoter areas) one hospital, of which the respective functions were to be as follows:

The health clinics were to perform simple curative and preventive tasks on a local basis. They were to treat common diseases and minor ailments, perform ante-natal examinations, detect illnesses such as malnutrition, educate mothers in the elements of infant and child health, teach the local population about hygiene, cleanliness in the preparation of food, the need for a balanced diet. So important is the educative function of the clinic that even the clinic building itself 'should be maintained at a high standard of hygiene as an example to the local community'.[12]

Medical personnel are scarce in Africa, and hence the clinics were to be staffed not by doctors but by trained medical auxiliaries. By carrying preventive services into the community and the home, they were to help to reduce the future demand for curative medicine. Again, by vetting cases locally and referring only those which they could not treat themselves with simple drugs and equipment, they were to help to ration the scarce skills of the highly qualified. This is a more economical use of resources than for the sick to queue up at out-patient clinics, and it prevents the hospitals from being swamped with improper demands which cannot but waste their time.

The health clinics are important information-gathering organs: 'The staff of the health unit should know the habits of the local people and observe and report any significant changes in the pattern of disease.'[13] They are also important in the formulation of policy, since the clinics are closely integrated both with local government and the local population. At the governmental level, the clinics often work in conjunction with other local services (such as sanitary and sewerage authorities, town planning and pest control authorities, agricultural schools) to satisfy local needs. Services such as good housing or the eradication of malaria are essential to a healthy environment and must link up with the work of the clinics. Again, the clinics work in close touch with the local community and reflect 'what the people themselves can do, individually and through collective programmes of self-help and community development, towards the improvement of health at

the level of the local community'.[14] Medicine is a community problem, and a developing health programme ought thus to enlist the
support of local movements for self-improvement.

Above the local health clinics in the hierarchy were to be the health
centres. Each centre was to provide continuous education and supervision for the medical auxiliaries staffing each of the five clinics in its
area. The director of each centre was to visit each clinic at least once a
fortnight, both for preventive purposes (say, to help plan immuni-
zation and health education campaigns) and in order to diagnose and
treat difficult cases (an activity partly curative in function, but also
partly educative insofar as it helps to train medical aides and thus
raises the standards of their future work). Difficult cases were to be
referred to the centres, which would have some beds available for
them. The general rule was to be this: 'The health centres, with their
satellite health clinics, and their links with area hospitals, should
further their aim to provide good medical care by becoming local
powerhouses of health education and preventive medicine. We see
them acting as demonstration and group teaching centres in healthier
living; consulting, advising and assisting local leaders and groups,
health workers and midwives in how to work with others in raising
levels of living.'[15]

Still higher in the hierarchy were to be the area hospitals. They were
to deal with more difficult cases that were referred to them from
below, and also to supervise the work of the health centres in their
area.

At the apex of the hierarchy were to be the Category 'A' hospitals
(no more than three in the whole country). These were to be large (500
beds or more) and each would not only serve as local general hospital
for its own area but would also act as reference hospital for a number
of health areas. Each was to have a staff of qualified consultant
specialists, who would regularly visit smaller hospitals to teach and
advise and could in an emergency even be called upon to give guidance
by radio to hospitals in isolated districts. In addition, each Category
'A' hospital was to set standards for other hospitals, partly by acting
as a postgraduate training centre, partly by accepting medical officers
from other hospitals for short periods to bring them up to date with
new developments and advances in their field.

In summary, the key concepts in the recommendations emerge as
referral, supervision, co-ordination, continuous education, prevention,
adequacy, and community medicine. Titmuss believed that the precondition for all of those proposals was a state system of medicine,

wherein resources were allocated on a national basis according to a plan formulated by the central government. It is interesting, however, that, although Titmuss obviously had no great love for private hospitals, he still did not call for the nationalization of voluntary agencies or regard it as essential for their integration into the system.

Third, there is the example of adequate blood for transfusion, another service that is not forthcoming in the American private enterprise system of health care.

The demand for blood in America is increasing rapidly, partly because of general sociological factors, partly as a result of advances in medical knowledge and technique. There is, for example, a higher incidence of road and industrial accidents, more urban violence, a rising percentage of the population over 65 and in need of proportionately more surgery. Then too, there are more haemophiliacs getting the blood they need; more 'poor risk patients' being accepted for surgical treatment; more open-heart and major cancer operations; more organ transplants. The supply of blood in America is, however, unfortunately not keeping pace with these new uses. As a result, chronic shortages of fresh blood now exist in most places. In New York, for example, 'operations are postponed daily' because of the 'acute and chronic shortage of blood',[16] and elective operations are often scheduled with an eye to its availability.

The problem in America is that the crude utilitarianism of the private market has failed to establish a satisfactory equilibrium. Blood appears to have a low price elasticity of supply, since substantial monetary incentives (to say nothing of trading stamps, tickets to baseball games, or discounts on prison sentences) are evidently inadequate to attract sufficient donors. Moreover, here too there can be failures of co-ordination such that blood might be expiring in one hospital (and thus being wasted by not being used within its 21-day life-span) while at the same time non-availability of blood could be causing an operation to be postponed in a neighbouring institution.[17] Naturally, such a shortage of blood is an infringement of the patient's freedom of choice. It reduces his freedom to have an essential operation, and possibly even to go on living.

Market forces curtail freedom in the area of blood. State intervention extends it. In Britain, blood is a valuable commodity but, because of the system of voluntary donorship, a commodity without price. Yet, unlike the situation in America, in Britain 'there is no shortage of blood. It is freely donated by the community for the community. It is a free gift from the healthy to the sick irrespective of income, class, ethnic group, religion, private patient or public patient. Since the National Health Service was established the quantity of blood issued to hospitals has risen by 265 per cent.'[18] In the same period (1948–67) the total population of England and Wales rose by 12%.[19] Moreover, 'the number of blood donations per 100 potential donors rose steadily from 1.8 in 1948 to 6.0 in 1968.'[20] The increase has been orderly and sustained, and an increased supply has at all times been forthcoming to meet an increased demand. Clearly, it is economically inefficient to treat human blood as a consumer good to be purchased from commercial sellers: other affluent and mobile societies such as America, Japan, Sweden and Russia do so, and have shortages as a result.

It makes sense, Titmuss argued, to rely on altruism rather than on commercialization, and to recognize that blood is not simply an economic good. In Britain, because of the system of voluntary donation and the suppression of the cash nexus, the response rate is good and the supply predictable and adequate. Altruism is capable of doing the job; private enterprise demonstrably is not.

Not only is more blood forthcoming in Britain than in America, but existing stocks are more effectively utilized. The 21-day life-span of blood, combined with the fact that it is unhealthy for donors to give blood too often, suggests not only the need for a wider network of donors but also that efficient use should be made of limited supplies. This in Britain is ensured by central co-ordination of blood supplies.

Scarcity of blood is a microsociological as well as a macrosociological phenomenon. Here again the British system is seen to be superior. A patient may count on receiving blood in Britain who in America would not even have been able to afford treatment in the first place. An American haemophiliac, who may require a vast quantity of blood for as simple an operation as the removal of a tooth, is a bad risk and finds it difficult to arrange private medical insurance, at least at a price he can afford to pay. A British haemophiliac, on the other hand, receives blood as a free gift from strangers and is not separated from it by a payment barrier which may appear insuperable (as when there is more than one haemophiliac in the family). A British haemophiliac, as Titmuss so eloquently puts it, 'would not wish to emigrate'.[21]

Unmet needs, when met rather than ignored, increase pressure on the community's resources; but they may also increase social felicity. This reminds us of the basic fallacy in the liberal theory of supply and demand, namely that it takes high prices and high profits to be the best index of need. This approach reflects such factors as the distribution of income, and thus fails to indicate that the quantity supplied of a good for which there is no effective demand (i.e. a good demanded by those unable to pay for it) may be sub-optimal compared with the goals and targets that society as a group has set itself.

Consider, for example, how property speculation has forced land values and rentals to prohibitive heights: 'Private enterprise is only building about 1,000 new dwellings a year in the county of London . . . . . and most of these are luxury flats for the rich.'[22] In such a case, quantity supplied is not only deficient but patently out of line with the needs of the society as a whole; and there is much to be said for *dirigisme* if it can at the very least hold at bay 'the predatory vulgarities of land speculators and property developers.'[23] Another example is the slums or immigrant areas which tend even now to be under-doctored,[24] although they in fact have an acute need for high-quality professionals so as to integrate the poor and the coloured with the rest of their fellow-citizens. Here reliance on the invisible hand of the market mechanism would make the situation worse, not better. What is needed is planning with a view to the satisfaction of social as well as simply individual needs. Only through planning of resource allocation can the quantity society thinks ought to be available of a particular good be put at the disposal of those who society feels ought to enjoy it.

14 The Failure of the Market IV: Price

America in the 1950s and 1960s spent a higher percentage of her Gross National Product on medical care than did Britain. This fact does not, however, demonstrate that the quality of service in America was better, or that the quantity supplied was greater. It might simply reflect rising cost to the consumer: 'Since 1948 it has risen much more than in Britain . . . . . By far the steepest rise has been registered by the price of hospital rooms and group hospital insurance premiums. These are now rising at the rate of over 7 per cent per year, or twice as fast as the national income.'[1]

American medicine is expensive and is experiencing rapid price inflation compared with the general cost-of-living index. The reasons, Titmuss indicated, were not chiefly to be sought on the side of demand (the argument that medical care is a good with a high income elasticity) but rather on the side of supply. Five examples will help to make this clear:

First, there is lack of co-ordination among private hospitals in the United States, and many suffer as a result from under-utilization of plant: 'One part of the price of non-planning – a 26 per cent average non-occupancy rate in short-term general hospital beds in 1957 – cost American consumers $3.5 billion in idle investment and $625 million in operating costs.'[2] The duplication of expensive and sophisticated equipment in these hospitals suggests wasteful maldistribution of resources; and there is also the point that, because of the 'technical rationale for large units',[3] small, profit-making hospitals experience diseconomies of scale which are ultimately translated into higher prices charged to the consumer and into slower national growth rates caused by misallocation of scarce resources.

Second, there is the administrative waste that results from parallel bureaucracies in the private sector. In the economic pluralism of the

American corporate free enterprise system, it is the consumer who pays for these multiplied inefficiencies of organization. In the case of private provision of blood, for instance, the consumer must pay for all the waste in the system, including 'an immense and swollen bureaucracy required to administer a complex banking system of credits, deposits, charges, transfers and so forth.'[4] And as for medical insurance: 'The administrative and commission costs of insurance companies for individual policies rose from 42 per cent in 1948 to 52 per cent in 1958. The consumer now gets less than half his dollar back in medical care.'[5] British experience confirms the inefficiency of private provision in the field of insurance: 'The administrative costs of private Workmen's Compensation Insurance were of the order of 30 to 40 per cent of the premiums collected. Such figures can now be compared with the administrative costs of the Department of Health and Social Security in administering the present system of National Insurance against Industrial Injuries and Diseases. These costs are in the neighbourhood of 5 to 10 per cent. The private market was many times more costly in terms of administrative efficiency.'[6]

Bureaucratization is a term which the mass media almost exclusively utilize in reference to the state sector. To Titmuss, however, as to Max Weber, the term involved the hierarchical structure of *any* large organization, public or private. Titmuss went further and argued that, given that bureaucracies are a fact of modern life, at least state bureaucracies have the advantage of cost-efficiency. There is more co-ordination in the state sector, less duplication of administrative and computer overheads, no selling and advertising costs. There is substantial saving of resources due simply to the fact that the doctor in Britain does not need to enquire into the financial means of each patient, send in bills, file suits for non-payment or absorb bad debts.

Titmuss deplored the waste involved in private sector bureaucracies, as the following economystic jeremiad reminds us: 'How much longer are we to be burdened with the heavy and wasteful administrative costs (to say nothing of the misuse of computer time) of the chaos of something like 60,000 private pension schemes?'[7]

Third, there is the financial cost to the consumer of the breakdown in the doctor-patient relationship. In America, doctors take out expensive insurance policies against malpractice suits and attempt to pass the high cost of the premiums on to the patient. Moreover, insurance companies protect themselves by obliging doctors to do tests and are a significant cause of unnecessary consultations and hospitalization, such 'defensive medical practice' being, of course, at the cost of the patient. Again, the doctor may waste resources on unnecessary treatment due to the lure of financial return; and may concentrate on curative medicine (in which he has a vested interest) to the detriment of preventive (in which he does not). The incidence of hepatitis too imposes a financial cost on the sufferer and his family and gives him a sensation of misplaced trust. Indeed, once the patient loses confidence in his doctor and comes to see that the parties are linked by a profit-oriented commodity transaction rather than the provision of a service governed by a disinterested professional ethic, there is more likely to be hostility, litigation, and hence a further financial cost.

Fourth, there is the high cost of blood to recipients who have to purchase it for money (those, for example, who do not repay in blood under the terms of blood-replacement schemes).

The cost of blood supplied to the patient in the United States is 5-15 times higher than in Britain.[8] Partly this is because American blood is regarded as a consumer good to be bought and sold at whatever price the traffic will bear, and must be purchased from donors at competitive prices (or from profit-oriented blood-banks and pharmaceutical companies). By offering a high price, private enterprise also lures away would-be voluntary donors, who can no longer afford the opportunity cost of altruism.

Partly too the high cost of blood in America reflects administrative waste occasioned by lack of co-ordination between a plurality of bureaucracies. About 15-30% of all blood collected in the United States is lost through outdating (due to its perishability at the end of 21 days)[9], a multi-million dollar annual loss but one which is to be expected in a system where in 1966-8 there were some 9,000 individual blood-banks concerned with collecting blood from donors.[10] Central co-ordination in Britain both allows for effective mobilization of existing supplies of blood and eliminates wasteful duplication of facilities and administrative staff. It also allows for the planning for the short-term demand curve. In England and Wales, only about 2 per cent of blood collected is wasted through inefficiency; in America the figure is possibly ten times as high.[11]

Then too, blood in America is expensive because of wasteful practices in the hospitals. Blood is squandered on 'defensive medical practice'; on medically unjustified surgery (such as an unnecessary appendectomy) motivated purely by the doctor's love of profit; and on supplementary treatment where the patient is infected with hepatitis in the course of a transfusion (a costly externality, as the patient must pay for the further services of scarce professionals and for expensive days in hospital as well as for still more blood). Blood is often the object of deliberate over-ordering by physicians (who prefer waste to shortage) and of hoarding by hospitals (who believe that 'blood loaned is gone forever'[12] and prefer waste to sharing).

Finally, blood in America is expensive because of international competition to obtain a scarce commodity. Blood and plasma are sold to the highest bidder, and hence there is substantial export from the United States to other countries (such as Sweden and Japan) where social growth (as approximated by the index of voluntary donorship) has lagged behind economic growth and a blood-shortage has emerged as a result.

Paradoxically, the high cost of blood makes America seem a richer country. Waste boosts American GNP figures, since stocks of blood are stocks like any other and since commercialization of blood transfusion systems converts an unpaid into a paid activity. Even the wasted services of the hospital used in treating induced cases of hepatitis are included in the GNP. What is excluded is the social cost. Yet the unquantifiable effects on family life of, say, permanent dependency of the recipient on the state because of a transfusion involving polluted blood have a significant social value, despite the fact that they have no market price.

Fifth, there is in the United States a 'trend from domiciliary to hospital care',[13] due to the declining importance of community medicine and the local G.P. In America, private, specialized medical care has 'built-in professional and financial preferences for institutional care'.[14] The patient is likely to be sent straight to a profit-making hospital, geared more often than not to short-stay patients and a high turnover. Needless to say, such treatment is expensive. Here as elsewhere, the privately produced article is inferior and simply cannot stand up to the competition of the social services.

15　Part Four: an Evaluation

Economics is concerned with the allocation of scarce goods and services among a plethora of alternative uses. Its methodology is individualist, it postulates the randomness of ends, and it assumes the whole is equal to the sum of the parts. It is liberal and utilitarian in its outlook, and places particular value on the way in which the household or firm votes in the unrestricted market-place.

Political economy, on the other hand, is anthropocentric rather than reiocentric in approach. It regards the production, distribution and exchange of goods and services as a bundle of social facts, and thus both as forming part of a wider matrix of social facts and as necessitating explanation in terms of other social facts. It recognizes the organic existence of society as a reality *sui generis*; stresses that ends are more often than not prescribed for the individual by social mores and behaviour patterns and hence are part of a social system rather than accidents of choice; and argues that many goods and services must be consumed collectively or not at all. Political economy emphasizes that the group as a whole must often make decisions as a crew concerning the direction in which it wishes to row; and it consequently lays particular stress on the voting patterns of the individual with respect to politicians, political parties and political programmes.

Richard Titmuss employed the interdisciplinary and normative methodology of political economy with a vigour and a rigour that must serve as an outstanding example of science in the service of society. He had to do so; for not only was he attempting to pioneer new territory by working out for himself a viable human-oriented theory of resource allocation, he was also continuously fighting a rearguard action against a savage army of Economic Men who accused him of lacking any real understanding of inputs and outputs.

It would be good to report that the philosopher of compassion and kindness succeeded in playing Tamburlaine to the Custers of profit and interest. It is sad to report that he did not, and this basically because his model of men and things omits adequate analysis of four fundamental variables: scarcity, choice, growth and pattern maintenance. In this chapter we shall examine each of these variables in turn.

(a) *Scarcity*. Titmuss recognized, at least in the case of Tanganyika, that where resources are not available in infinitely elastic supply there is a need for social policy to be realistic: 'The more limited the total resources available, the greater the need to husband those resources carefully; to order priorities in the right balance, and to set clear objectives for the future.'[1]

So aware was Titmuss of the extreme scarcity of resources in Africa that he joined with his colleagues in opposing universal state medical insurance. Health insurance should be introduced, but only in areas with relatively well-developed medical services, and the reason was this: 'We expect that the introduction of such a scheme, even if contributions were limited to employers, would result in heavier demands for medical attention. It would not be right, in our view, to introduce a scheme and to lead certain sections of the population to expect to claim better medical care if the resources and staff to meet such demands are not available. In general, then, the development of a health insurance scheme should march in step with area improvements in medical resources.'[2] Otherwise, standards of service would fall; and 'this should not be allowed to happen.'[3]

Because of the existence in Africa of a severe resources constraint, Titmuss accepted the utility of the price barrier as a gatekeeper in a situation where all wants cannot be met nor all needs satisfied. Health charges, after all, were the key to quality consultations in the proposals he and his associates made in Tanganyika. There the problem was simply this: 'The more cases any medical worker is expected to see and treat in a day, the less time can be given to each and the less the value of the service given.'[4] In order to defend the value of consultations, some way had to be found to limit demand; and the recommendation made was for charges to be introduced. Of course, so as not to frighten away the poor (who probably most needed attention) these charges were to be moderate and there were to be exceptions: thus ante-natal care was to be free, and fees were to be waived for the indigent at the discretion of the staff of health centre, clinic or hospital (such discretion being necessary in the absence of any other viable means of identifying the poor). Nonetheless, and with these exceptions, fees were to be payable.

Titmuss recommended the application of user-charges in Tanganyika. He did not, however, see fit to make similar recommendations in his own country. Naturally, Britain is not a poor country experiencing the same sort of absolute scarcity as is to be found in less developed nations; but relative affluence is not irrefutable evidence that the price mechanism is obsolete. The price mechanism, after all, performs three vital functions in the market sector with such efficacy as to suggest its extension rather than its suppression in the world of welfare, particularly in view of the fact that Titmuss nowhere satisfactorily explains how in its absence its three vital functions are to be fulfilled. These three vital functions are as follows:

First, deterrence of excessive demand. If the consumer had to bear the cost of a service himself, he might demand less of it (witness the fact that, as Titmuss was aware, the introduction of charges for dentures and spectacles in 1951 and of more extended charges in 1952 both raised revenue and 'had some effect in reducing demand'[5]); and harnessing the negative correlation between changes in price and changes in quantity demanded might thus be a useful means of allocating scarce supplies and preventing misuse of resources. Were at least some welfare to be rationed by price, consumers might come to think of a visit to the doctor (to ask about a hangover) in terms of nine pints of best bitter foregone, and might demand less marginal treatment if a genuine sacrifice had to be made in exchange for the benefit.

Titmuss' system is one of rationing by need and by right; but where there is a resources constraint such a system all too often becomes one of rationing by availability of a free good in limited supply. Titmuss hardly mentions long waiting-times, overworked doctors, over case-loaded social workers, lightning consultations, *ad hoc* means tests, all of which are both indices of scarcity and *de facto* mechanisms of allocation; and he brushes aside the consumer frustration and cynicism which must inevitably arise in a second-best situation where all simply cannot adequately be accommodated, and where rising social expectations are making the bottleneck worse, not better. Given scarcity, moreover, priorities and criteria must be established by welfare professionals (an élite which may or may not be in touch with the collective mind), and this can involve a form of stigma that Titmuss did not envisage: should professionals decide, for instance, that training colleges for the young should enjoy a superior ranking to geriatric wards for the old, the old (who for economic reasons are condemned to receive inferior treatment) may well feel rejected and unwelcome pariahs. Such a feeling could be avoided were there to be rationing by price in the welfare sector.

In Titmuss' defence it must be noted that rationing by price effectively eliminates those least able to pay; and that for this reason over-utilization of facilities is morally superior to under-utilization. It must also be noted that Titmuss was attempting to apply the philosophy of the political market (where one man has one vote) to the conditions of the economic market (where a rich man has more votes than a poor man), and was hence seeking to establish a truly democratic society as he conceived it to be. It must nonetheless be noted that scarcity exists; and that if the housewife were offered fish fillets at the same price as she now pays for her mixture and her tablets, the fishing industry would almost certainly grow as fat as the drug industry is today, unless fish were to be strictly rationed by professionals on whom more often than not the ultimate check is only the judgement of other like-minded men.

Second, information-collection. The market mechanism prices goods and services so as to charge all the traffic will bear and measures changes in intensity of needs through changes in profits. It thus enables the consumer to reveal and register his preferences concerning the quality, quantity and kind of commodity he desires. It is a valuable source of information on what people want, since it sensitively and impersonally records the choices they elect to make.

The welfare sector in the Titmuss model is emancipated from the market mechanism; and this suggests a real danger that the information gathered (on, say, the kind of education desired by parents for their children in school, or the kind of treatment desired by children for their parents in hospital) will be scarce and imprecise, and more likely to reflect the views of professionals, politicians and administrators than of the inarticulate and passive mass of takers. The collectivity cannot always know what the individual consumer desires without asking him (as the market does); and moreover, the corporatist ideal of a general will and a group interest in caring for the dependent presupposes an exceptionally delicate value judgement as to who needs care and as to what sort of care society *sui generis* believes he ought to have.

Titmuss nowhere adequately explains how a society is in practice to determine the optimal rather than the minimal provision of a free good, or faces up to the fact that there are often a multitude of ways to deal with the same human wants and needs. There are a number of possible menus for meals-on-wheels and a number of ways to furnish hostels for the destitute; and while a doctor arguably knows best how to treat gangrene and malaria, the local council does not necessarily know best how to house the elderly, how to design low-cost flats, or how to cope with the plight of battered wives (whose demands for women's lib are more likely to be met with librium than with liberation).

There is also a point about standards. Titmuss' examples of egalitarianism tend to concern levelling up. Giving the average consumer what he is used to, however, can also mean a democratic vote in favour of levelling down. The wealthy accountant whisked into a National Health hospital may miss his juicy steak and his glass of port, and may deeply regret the fact that because he is ill and integrated he is no longer able to vote with his pocketbook against thin soup and pigs' trotters. Nonetheless, such equality, because it takes the form of the trotters rather than the steak, does have the latent function of economizing on scarce resources.

Third, comparison and co-ordination of alternative ends. Two commodities in the market sector can be compared in terms of the amount of money the consumer is prepared to sacrifice in order to acquire each. Two commodities in the welfare sector cannot be compared in the same way, since the marginal sacrifice involved in both purchases is nil. And, by extension, two commodities, one in each sector, cannot either be compared, since one is deterrently dear while the other is temptingly free.

Understandably, in a mixed economy where one good is an exchange and the other a gift, it is difficult for the consumer to make meaningful adjustments at the margin. He cannot decide, for example, suddenly to spend £100 more on a colour television and £100 less on the care he receives in hospital, but must accept decisions made on his behalf by others. This reduces the individual's freedom to spend his own money as he sees fit (a point advocates of laissez-faire have not been slow to stress), and it also reduces the sensitivity of the two-sector model. It is, after all, virtually impossible for policy-makers to make direct comparisons between the market and the welfare sectors since their success-indicators are so different; and Titmuss provides no discussion of those forms of utilitarian calculus as might serve as a common denominator (such as cost-benefit analysis or other approaches to cost-effectiveness of investment in the public sector). Even in *Income Distribution and Social Change* he avoids the choice and use of a discounting rate of interest altogether, evidently regarding it as market-tainted and irrelevant in the world of social policy. Irrelevant it may be, but its absence causes an information gap to remain in his model due to the lack of robust comparative inter-sectoral indicators. Were welfare to be flexibly priced, of course, then that information gap would disappear, as the subjectively determined trade-off between the two sectors would as a result become instantaneously quantifiable.

The price mechanism has a general as well as a partial equilibrium function insofar as it ensures the co-ordination of a multitude of discrete markets; the mixed economy carries in itself the potential property of being badly mixed, and Titmuss is to be criticized for not explaining how his two sectors were to be integrated into one whole. Implicit, of course, is full-scale economic planning, in view of Titmuss' belief in the efficacy of strong governmental action and direction (and in this context we may note his optimistic announcement in 1966 despite the fact that it has with hindsight a bitterly ironical ring to the reader: 'Now that the Government has begun to lay a sounder basis for a higher rate of growth in the future after inheriting a decade or more of incompetence and dereliction it is, I think, more rather than less likely that our economic targets will be broadly attained.'6) Surprisingly, however, Titmuss had little to say about precisely what form that planning was to take; and was conveniently able for that reason neatly to sidestep the potential trade-off between manpower and welfare planning on the one hand and individual freedom on the other. There can, after all, be a serious conflict between one man's desire to study metaphysics and society's general will to equip itself with skilled engineers; and in such a case the would-be philosopher might deeply resent co-ordination by plan and even desperately seek to pay a higher price for the right to study the self-indulgent and unproductive subject of his choice. He will seek in vain in an educational system founded on social plan rather than individual preference, in a world where 'all social services are allocative systems and ration demand and supply.'7 Of course they are; and that, he will reason with all the intellectual rigour of the skilled engineer, is the very source of his bitterness and frustration.

(b) *Choice*. Titmuss notes that hospitals in Britain have not always appreciated that 'courtesy and sociability have a therapeutic value'8 but relates this deplorable fact to the fragmentation of services and extensive professionalization that arise within the hierarchy of a closed institution. It could also be argued, however, that this deplorable fact is but the symptom of a much deeper social malady, namely that the client in the welfare state has had inadequate opportunity to choose; and that when a man becomes a patient rather than a consumer, he falls victim to a multitude of professional insensitivities caused not by excessive specialization but by inadequate competition. Where welfare professionals compete for sovereign consumers, the individual has in his own feet the power to vote against rudeness: he can apply economic sanctions by taking his business to another shop. Where welfare professionals do not compete for sovereign consumers, the individual has no alternative to the posture of the taker rather than the chooser; and such humiliation may well prove not simply a limitation of his freedom but a threat to his self-respect and sense of initiative as well. *Coercive soc. worker.*

Titmuss placed a high valuation on choice within the welfare state. Yet his commitment to the principle of universalism made him blind to some valuable alternative forms of state intervention which might substantially expand the range of choices open to the consumer. Chief among these is the case of welfare vouchers. Under such a system the state might elect to reprivatize the health, educational and accommodation services into a number of small, competitive purveyors, and then give families vouchers to spend on the doctor, school or flat of their choice. These vouchers could be graduated according to income, so as to give more ear-marked income-maintenance to those families most in need of it; and they could, of course, be supplemented out of the family budget, thereby allowing customers if they so wish to express their involvement in a particular service by directing funds to welfare which in a 'free-on-demand system might have gone on bingo.

Welfare vouchers would fill two important gaps in the Titmuss model of welfare and society: *VOUCHER SYS ADVOCA*

First, by breaking the link between finance and provision, by *Persmar* stimulating welfare merchants to compete for welfare business while simultaneously equipping welfare customers with the wherewithal to *Virtue* pay, they encourage pluralism, diversity, dispersion of power and *of mkt* greater sensitivity to the wishes of the consumer. A Jewish father could send his son to a Jewish school where the teachers wear hats, a Catholic father could send his son to a Catholic school where the teachers wear cassocks, a progressive father could send his son to a progressive school where the teachers wear nothing at all, and each could vote with his vouchers for the unique kind of education he prefers. Similarly, a woman patient might be prepared to supplement her vouchers out of her savings in order to be sure of treatment by female doctors in an uneconomically small local hospital reserved exclusively for women; and there is no moral or social reason why she should not be allowed to do so.

Vouchers mean an end to coerced conformity and stimulate tolerance of multiple life-styles. They also make the receipt of welfare itself less stigmatizing; for automatic state supplementation of income is in such a system both universal (we all receive some vouchers in identical sealed envelopes) and impersonal (not at the discretion of the faceless bureaucrat nor at the initiative of the timid beneficiary).

Second, welfare vouchers provide a solution to the problem of integrated accommodation, a problem so complex that it is conspicuous in Titmuss' work by its almost complete absence.

The situation at present is that the council estate is chiefly reserved for problem families with a high number of 'points', and is thus far from representing the mixed and balanced community that is to be found in the surgical or maternity wards of a large state hospital. This means in turn that the local comprehensive school is not truly comprehensive since its neighbourhood catchment area is not a typical cross-section of the national family.

Housing vouchers would replace the ghettoes of the council estate by a system of rent-subsidies paid on a sliding scale to householders, thus enabling poorer families to live in similar houses and streets to those in which wealthier families choose to dwell: after all, the less privileged have ever-widening reference groups and may as result feel relatively deprived if given an egg-box in the sky rather than a self-respectable semi-detached. Indeed, home-ownership (financed through voucher-subsidized mortgage repayments offered to families rejected by building societies) may itself be a source of considerable pride and dignity. Housing vouchers, in short, could prove a useful technique for mixing neighbourhoods as well as closing the vast gap in the area of housing between actual supply and potential demand; and could at the very least provide that technique for the social allocation of dwellings which Titmuss himself never really supplied.

Such a system of vouchers would, of course, have been anathema to Titmuss, who would vociferously have attacked it on three grounds. Unfortunately, none of the three objections is entirely satisfactory or fully convincing:

First, Titmuss would have argued that vouchers mean re-privatization and reprivatization means waste. Yet his case against the private sector is not always fair. He argues in one place, for example, that the American purchaser of medical insurance gets back less than half his dollar in the form of care and only later notes that this is true exclusively for individual policies, the benefits for group policies being as much as 90% of contributions.[9] And elsewhere he compares the efficiency of the private sector insurance industry in the 1930s with the efficiency of public sector social security in the 1960s without troubling to point out that the gap of thirty years almost certainly makes the data non-comparable.[10]

Titmuss does not adequately distinguish between those needs that the private market *does not* satisfy (such as the need for plentiful health care in poor areas) and those needs that the private market *cannot* satisfy (such as the need for the social integration of the indigent through the use of common institutions); and tends falsely to regard social services as by their very nature public goods. A public good (say, Hampstead Heath or Loch Lomond) must be made available to all if it is to be made available to any; a social service can be allocated by price, by a special tax levied at the moment of consumption and on the beneficiary alone. Titmuss tends to confuse the proposition that the special tax *should not* be levied (a perfectly valid ethical judgement) with the proposition that the special tax *cannot* be levied (an economic argument belied, to return to our example of health care in the ghettos, by techniques such as vouchers which Titmuss deliberately chose to ignore); and it is possibly for this reason that he says so little about regulatory legislation to curb the worst excesses of unbridled private enterprise in the field of welfare. Consider, for example, the case of private sector pensions: if non-transferable now they could be made transferable in the future, survivor's rights could be guaranteed, individual risk-rating could be expanded, consumers could be more fully informed of their rights and alternatives. The law of the land could in short replace the law of the jungle without the need for full socialized provision of the services in question; and it is hence misleading to present the argument in terms of a Manichean *Legisl* choice between public provision and private chaos. Commercial banks which trade in money are licensed and screened to prevent anti-social sharp practices; there is no economic reason why commercial banks which trade in blood could not be treated similarly.

Just as Titmuss was on occasion excessively pessimistic about the private sector, so his case in favour of the welfare state is at times excessively rosy. He argues that there is no shortage of blood for transfusion in the United Kingdom without noting that this view is hardly held by all members of the medical profession; overestimates the extent to which adequate information is in reality disclosed to the community by social security and other welfare authorities; and has a

somewhat idealized picture of the degree to which the general practitioner is today a sympathetic family friend rather than merely the
local technocrat with a penchant for placebo. He plays down the
frequency with which the most satisfactory solution is rejected by the
welfare authorities as too expensive; underestimates the incidence of
abuse in the public sector (as where consultants have in the past seen
private patients on National Health time and even premises at the cost
of their public patients); and fails to note the crucial role played by
private philanthropic and voluntary organizations in coping with the
multiple diswelfares that seep through the public safety-net (such
charities being nowadays as likely to be run by hairy hippies who
know where it's at and wish they were there as by the traditional blue
ladies with blue hats). All in all, Titmuss is not fully successful in
driving forth his enemies with the jawbone of an ass; for he does not in
the last analysis convincingly demonstrate either that private is typically bad or that public is typically good.

Second, Titmuss would have argued that vouchers mean a multiple
and differentiated standard of service and a consequently malintegrated society, thus negating the very *raison d'être* of social policy. Yet
the fact is that the objective of encouraging integration and discouraging alienation is in a world of market, class, power and hedonism too
ambitious a function for a handful of social services; and that it is
doubtful whether welfare can truly foster a sense of community,
compassion, citizenship, common fate, common identity where no
such subjective perceptions would otherwise exist.

It could be maintained, however, that even if social policy does not
significantly represent integration–furtherance (even if Titmuss grossly
overestimated its utility in the process of social engineering), it
nonetheless retains the vital function of coping with chronic distress
and unrelieved dependency. This suggests in turn that scarce resources
should be concentrated on those who need them most, and that, in
order to prevent the butter of welfare from being spread too thin,
those who are able to pay for such services as education and health
should be encouraged to do so. If universalism does not mean integration (and if the means test does not mean stigma), then universalism to some extent means waste, since it ensures that benefits
will be provided free of charge to many affluent recipients who do
have the wherewithal to pay school-fees and prescription charges.

Such recipients might indeed be keen to pay if offered diversity and
variety in place of assimilation and uniformity; for they might believe
that the individual remains the best judge of what is desirable for

himself and his family, and might regard the tyranny of the majority as tyranny nonetheless. Such recipients might perceive that, carried to its logical conclusion, lack of choice of flat (as of school or of hospital, Titmuss' more usual but misleadingly selective examples) must result if the social services are to submerge divisive differences in the bliss of a shared situation. Such recipients might deny that alienation from the national family is tantamount to alienation from oneself, one's relatives and one's friends; and might even reproach Titmuss for attempting to define social policy in terms of virtually one subjective perception, which, in their view, it neither can nor ought to generate.

Third, Titmuss would have argued that vouchers impose an insuperable administrative burden, particularly if allocated on a means-tested basis (as they must be if the rich are not to have a monopoly of superior schools and private beds in hospitals). Here it can only be noted that Titmuss exaggerated the administrative difficulties of means–tested schemes in order to make it appear that that which must be consciously chosen by a community is also thrust upon it by the insuperable deficiencies of science.

The administration of welfare vouchers is, of course, a costly process. That cost need not, however, represent a net drain on national resources, as it would at least in part be offset by two countervailing forces: first, there would be the repatriation of existing civil servants from newly reprivatized areas of the welfare complex and, second, there would be a reduced demand for state-financed welfare from the rich (particularly if their demands for reduced contributions as the counterpart of reduced benefits are not proportionately met, forcing them even further to supplement their vouchers out of funds that would otherwise have been diverted to private consumption).

(c) *Growth*. Titmuss welcomed both economic growth and the welfare state and evidently regarded them as complementary one to the other. A growing economy, after all, benevolently generates a growing mass of tax revenues available to be ploughed back into the welfare infrastructure; while meanwhile the welfare state generously feeds growth by providing schools, hospitals and equality of opportunity (the latter a 'democratic precondition of faster economic growth'[11], partly because it supplies trained manpower and partly because it promotes integration and represses resentment). Titmuss chose, however, to neglect at least three cases in which a definite antithesis might obtain between the social services and economic growth, and which demonstrate the existence of a potential trade-off between the social and the economic:

First, imbalance. Titmuss believed that welfare should be regarded as desirable in its own right quite apart from the contribution it made to the national economy (the justification for good pensions as an alternative to compulsory euthanasia); and for this reason it is regrettable that he never specified the ideal balance between public and private sectors, or even suggested a basis on which a direct comparison could be made. Welfare is expensive; and a country needs to ensure a correct balance between productive and non-productive activities if it is to be successful in the creation of wealth and in the export of that wealth to foreign nations in exchange for those investment and consumer goods which it wishes to import. Particularly since Britain is a highly open economy, the question of the maximal share in the national income that can be diverted to those forms of public spending not directly complementary to the process of wealth-creation becomes one of crucial importance. A comprehensive theory of social policy needs to recognize that welfare (both absolutely and relatively) cannot be expanded indefinitely; and needs to specify (as Titmuss does not) exactly how much non-complementary welfare a given country at a given point in time can afford to consume.

Second, the professional ethic. Titmuss recommended that the doctor be included in the welfare sector, arguing that the doctor has a shaky professional ethic and is unlikely to provide truthful information and optimal care in market conditions. Titmuss did not, however, recommend that the lawyer and the accountant be similarly rescued from the corrosion of their professional ethic in the cold waters of competition. Yet, as Durkheim reminds us, occupational *anomie* can strike any group of professionals once collective sentiments become weak and moral fibre breaks down. Indeed, the truthlessness of the shopkeeper and the hidden persuader, the slovenly and shoddy workmanship of the plumber and carpenter, the zeal of the repairman to replace parts that have not worn out, all suggest that Titmuss' case against the market sector is incomplete; and that a multitude of other groups beyond simply the profit-maximizing medical men might need state protection from themselves in order to reduce the waste of the nation's scarce resources. Titmuss is being unfair in trying to have it both ways: it is analytically unsatisfactory simply to say that those groups now in the welfare state need help in preserving their fragile ethic while those groups now in the market sector do not. The philosopher needs also to explain why this is so;

and such an explanation Titmuss, vague as usual on lines of de-marcation, omits to provide.

The argument concerning the relationship between waste and pro-fessional ethic can, of course, be reversed. It could be maintained that welfare professionals with security of tenure, a guaranteed income and little occassion for competition and rivalry will become sleepy and apathetic bureaucrats; and that society in such a situation does not get maximum output per unit of input precisely because the professional in the state sector faces a conflict of interest between ethic and repose no less real than he would have faced in the market sector between ethic and pay. The doctor's daily bread comes to him automatically, after all, whether or not he visits the marginal teenager with migraine on a snowy Christmas Eve.

Third, finance. The welfare state must be paid for, and on a more massive scale than if benefits were selective. But if the finance is to be provided through public sector borrowing of funds that would other-wise have been saved, then the net result is likely to be inflationary (and inflation is not just an immensely unfair redistributive mechanism but a serious impediment to economic growth as well). And if the finance is to be provided through taxation, then misallocation and disincentive are real possibilities.

The problem with taxation is this: if the state burdens the more productive and rewards the less productive, the material benefit to the community will be reduced if the more productive become disheartened and diminish their own productivity as result. Economists tend to regard the quantity supplied of an input as a function of its remuneration; and while this assumption may well be fallacious (since men work for prestige, power and job-satisfaction as well as pay, and may indeed increase the supply of their effort when taxes rise so as to restore previous standards of living), it is so widely accepted that the friend of taxation must make his own position clear and present alternative evidence. This Titmuss does not do; and the reader remains entitled to assume that narrowed differentials consequent on pro-gressive taxation will have a disincentive effect on labour supply, initiative, enterprise and efficiency (in the form of, say, a reduced propensity to stay on at school in order to acquire further qualifications; or in the form of a reluctance to seek promotion and greater responsibility at work; or in the form of a refusal to change jobs where the gross increment in pay is inviting and the net increment invisible). Here we have a case where there may be a blatant con-tradiction between equal opportunity and the incentive to take advantage of it; and yet a case of which Titmuss seems to be unaware.

paving Disincentive effects might also obtain in the market for savings (as where households are so discouraged by the high taxation of interest and dividends that they decide to put today's pleasure before tomorrow's) and for investment (as where firms are prevented by the high taxation of profits from expanding plant, even if this ultimately means worsening standards of service and reduced employment of labour at some time in the future). Understandably, such multiple disincentive effects throughout the economy might well add up to a slower rate of growth and thus to a smaller pool of resources available to finance welfare than had taxes been less penal in incidence; and Titmuss may hence justifiably be criticized for not saying how individuals and firms in his view are likely to respond to changes in taxation. This omission is particularly significant in view of the fact that he envisaged an increased role for direct taxation in the welfare world to come, since direct taxes kill two birds with one stone: they not only provide finance but help to moderate what Tawney described as 'violent contrasts of wealth and power'[12] and thus have an egalitarian as well as a purely fiscal function to fulfil.

Tawney accepted that income differentials should continue to exist, but urged that they should not be so great as to obscure men's common condition as equal citizens. His view that 'the extremes both of riches and poverty are degrading and anti-social'[13] had a profound influence on the Labour movement, and not least on Titmuss who almost four decades later echoed it as follows: 'History suggests that human nature is not strong enough to maintain itself in true community where great disparities of income and wealth preside.'[14] Neither philosopher, however, was eager to specify precisely how much planned redistribution of life-chances and incomes is required to ensure social integration. Neither, consequently, was compelled to face up to the fact that more inequality might be functionally necessary in the economic system than was dreamt of in his philosophy. This direct conflict between social and economic objectives is nowhere better illustrated than in the tragic case-history of Jack and Jill:

Jack, who lives amid the dinge, grot and tat of a subsidized empire on which the concrete never sets, is known to envy Jill her elegant flat in the King's Road and her week-end retreat on the banks of the Tees. Jack is heard to argue that Jill is only able to afford such superior accommodation because of her superior income; and that that superior income is not a functional reward at all but simply a rent or surplus which she is able to command because of her natural skill, talent, intelligence and aptitude, or because of her position in the traditional hierarchy of pay-structures. Jack is understood to propose that, since Jill would be willing to perform precisely the same work for a substantially smaller premium, the surplus should be captured for society by means of higher levels of progressive taxation.

Jack might naturally be correct in his diagnosis and justified in his recommendations. But in the particular case-history we are examining he is not; for he is here mistaking a functional reward for a genuine surplus and is here underestimating the extent to which Jill's income truly reflects her ambition, initiative, effort, her lengthy and arduous training, the overtime she is willing to work and the responsibility she is prepared to take on. If therefore in this case the state acts on Jack's information and puts up direct taxes (both to integrate Jack and to raise revenue), Jill might simply reduce the supply of her labour, while simultaneously feeling resentful both of Jack and of the state. Moreover, the avowed goals of increased taxation might not be attained: Jack might remain malintegrated (since some differentials survive and thus some inequalities at play in the quantity and quality of consumables continue to reinforce inequalities at work in power and prestige) and revenue might remain unraised (since slower economic growth means that the state cannot depend to the same extent on natural growth in public finance). Neither objective of increased taxation is here attained; and the logical next step (especially in a country with an ambitious welfare programme and a low average propensity to save) is likely to be even steeper tax-rates, which are in turn likely to alienate Jill still further and to reduce the supply of her effort still more.

The tragic case-history of Jack and Jill is but an anecdote. It is an anecdote, however, which illustrates a complex situation where the imperative to integrate clearly comes into conflict with the desire for economic growth. It is an anecdote, furthermore, which raises two fundamental questions to which Titmuss provides no satisfactory answer:

Firstly, are there no alternative modes of integration to that delimited by common services and progressive taxation?

Many philosophers have argued that, just as governmental intervention need not mean integration, so integration can well develop without it. When Jack and Jill exchange goods and services in the free market-place, for example, the feelings of interdependence, organic solidarity and reciprocal utility furtherance that result might truly bring them closer together than common welfare institutions ever could. Here we have a situation where social integration and economic growth are not contradictory precisely because even in the economic market man is a social animal, a situation the very existence of which Titmuss, as it happens, would have denied; for he consistently assumed monetary exchange to be economic in nature, acquisitive in objective, and thus in its very essence neither role-defining nor a source of fellowship. His distinction between economic man and social man is, however, untenable and spurious: both the reciprocal gifts of the Trobriand Islanders and the unilateral transfers of the modern British welfare state represent command over resources, while the utilitarian exchanges of the market sector play in practice an important part in the network of social interaction. This result is reassuring; for, in view of the central place occupied in most modern societies by working and earning, it is likely that if a sense of common fate is to be generated at all, it must originate with the independent and the active rather than with the unproductive and the marginal.

Titmuss would not have accepted that adequate social integration can be an unintended outcome of free enterprise capitalism. Nor, however, would he apparently have accepted the case for a far more socialist alternative to common services and progressive taxation, namely the planning of differentials. The argument for pay-policies in this context is simply that Jack and Jill would be more intimately integrated were income-structures to be insulated from the vagaries of collective bargaining (not least because the economic market unjustifiably redistributes the national income in favour of the strong union to the detriment of the weak); that it is vital for an impartial outsider to reassure Jack of the extent to which Jill's pay is not a surplus engendered by accident or tradition but a true functional reward; and that, in a world where men are judged by what they earn as well as by what they spend, wide differences in gross (pre-tax) incomes remain a divisive factor which even the most egalitarian tax system in the world cannot eliminate. So convincing is the argument for pay-policies that it is surprising to find in Titmuss' work a total neglect of the potential contribution which such policies could make to social integration. This neglect is particularly unfortunate in view of the fact that Titmuss himself provides no rigorous definition of economic justice which might serve as a countervailing theory to the market sector's definition in terms of marginal revenue productivity as approximated by observable differentials. Here as elsewhere Titmuss displays an amazing insensitivity to the problems of the independent, and grossly understates the case for the integration of healthy men as well as sick.

Secondly, in the hypothetical situation where the imperative to integrate does come into conflict with the desire for economic growth, would it be justifiable to resolve the conflict by declaring that baubles and trinkets are at the best of times phenomena of no great consequence?

Galbraith has argued that affluence in itself is of zero marginal utility where it only signifies that a country is rich in toys such as the toaster which prints an inspirational message on each piece of toast; and has warned of the degree to which the public sector suffers under the liability that it does not advertise services or create wants. Titmuss, however, appears not to have been a Galbraithian; for his model seems to imply not so much a critique of the false God of consumerdom as an attempt to enlarge the circle of participants permitted to worship at the shrine. Titmuss did not challenge the legitimacy of Jill's toaster; simply, he deeply regretted that Jack as well did not have one.

(d) *Pattern Maintenance.* The key word in Titmuss' vocabulary is integration. Yet, paradoxically, it is integration that is most conspicuously lacking in the world view with which he confronts us. On the one hand there is the market sector, dominated by the laws of supply and demand and governed by the norm of reciprocity of exchanges. On the other hand, however, there is the welfare sector, dominated by the need to avoid stigma (and to promote social integration, cover social disutilities, plan redistribution and allocate resources with optimal efficiency) and governed by the norm of unilaterality of transfers. A mixed economy is also a mixed society, and Titmuss may rightly be criticized for not clarifying the relationship between the two sectors which he evidently intended should co-exist side by side.

Titmuss postulated moral schizophrenia and recognized that the individual would have to adapt simultaneously to two quite different ways of life, one based on monetary exchanges and the other on free gifts. He also anticipated that the norm of unilaterality would in time spread out from the welfare sector until it came to embrace a wide range of human relationships, and was pleased to be able to confirm that, due to a 'fusion of intelligence and concern for social justice and equality', we are indeed already witnessing a 'growing power of altruism over egoism'[15]. Tragically, however, Titmuss almost certainly confused his own optimistic view of the world as it ought to be with a perhaps less glorious picture of the world as it is and is likely to become. In real life, as every child knows, the Sugar Plum Fairy is often danced off the stage by the King of the Rats; and, applied to the problems of welfare and society, this important result reminds us that moral schizophrenia may ultimately be transcended not by the triumph of altruism but by the victory of egoism.

Dependency, after all, is not man's permanent or natural state. It is simply a womb with a view out on to the spacious green pastures of independence, where acquisition and ambition, competition and comparison, profit and productivity gambol by the babbling brook, and where unbridled possessive individualism kicks its heels in the teeth of the *emptor* who forgets to *caveat*. In the market sector, where getting on means getting ahead, the values of welfareism would indeed prove a liability rather than an asset; for a businessman who stressed community and compassion and attempted to love his neighbour as himself would sell few cabbages and acquire a reputation for considerable eccentricity. Understandably, therefore, the welfare sector does not make a free gift of its values, and offers an ethos which must be consumed on the premises or not at all. Singularly lacking in self-confidence, the welfare sector recognizes that it has but a modest supportive role to play: it offers the climber a free bowl of hot soup and sends him forth to ascend new peaks. Should he then refuse to advance, the social worker is dispatched to encourage him to reform himself rather than his society; the doctor to discover the reasons for his neurotic and abnormal behaviour patterns; and the teacher to offer him a marketable skill such as might enable him at last to escape from his imprisonment in paradise.

Moreover, even when dependent most men find it difficult to see the essential difference between the two sectors; and tend to consume the services of the hospital in the same way as they consume the services of the television, in both cases in exchange for a pre-paid impost, in both cases as part of a mass public absorbing a standardized product produced with a view to maximum economies of scale. The fundamental moral problem is that people do not in practice feel significantly different in the realm of the sacred from the way they feel in the realm of the profane, and this is almost certainly because the welfare state to the ordinary citizen represents socialization of consuming but not of producing. Titmuss believed that the welfare state must be fraternalist, not paternalist; but he offered no examples apart from the gift of blood of actual cases where voluntary service to the community in fact developed once welfare rights were conferred. Because, moreover, he seriously underestimated the extent to which most people think of social services in terms of taking rather than in terms of giving (and neglected the well-known fact that people as consumers are in any case likely to vote themselves more of a free good than they as taxpayers are prepared to pay for), he no less seriously underestimated the extent to which most people regard taxation as a burden rather than a privilege. Perhaps sharing can be a source of deep satisfaction; but, since even Titmuss accepted the view of the Economic Men that consumption makes happy, it is not in itself obvious that the cost of Jack's spell in hospital will be more highly valued by Jill than the electric toothbrush or colour television on which she would otherwise have spent her money, or that she will be eager to write an open cheque in favour of unintegrated black pensioners saddled with social diswelfares dating back four centuries or more. There is, in short, no *a priori* reason to expect that generosity and the social sector will in future wax, or that selfishness and the private sector will wane; and so powerful is the lure of commodity consumption that there is some reason to expect the opposite to be the case.

Even welfare professionals, like the rest of us not always the men they ought to be, can be more guided by lust than by love. Titmuss misleadingly plays down the extent to which the values of the economic market are present in the social market and pays insufficient attention to the perceptions that welfare professionals in the real world actually have of themselves and their role. Thus it is both true and false (and therefore confusing) to say that there is no cash nexus between doctor and patient or between teacher and taught. It is true in the sense that the recipient of welfare personally parts with no cash in direct exchange for the benefit provided. It is, however, false in the sense that the purveyor of welfare makes his free gift to the recipient on the clear understanding that his bill will still be paid. Indeed, in such a limping welfare environment the bilateral transfer is so implicit that the doctor may be prepared to let the patient suffer and even die when he downs his tools in defence of a pay claim or to secure an overtime guarantee; while the teacher may be motivated to shut his shop altogether and take industrial action should the social worker jump the eternal queue and distort the traditional status hierarchy of pecuniary compensation. Such behaviour (the order of the day in the market sector) never fails to amaze in the world of welfare. It ought not to do so. Concern has its cost, care its price; for love is in truth the original scarce commodity.

16   Conclusion

Richard Titmuss regarded the National Health as a paradigm for the
national health but never fully worked out the details of a theory of
social responsibility which remains tantalisingly limited in scope; and
it must in the last analysis be concluded that, despite his pledge to be
generalist and interdisciplinary and to adopt a rigorous sociological
approach to problems of social welfare, his contribution nonetheless
lacks the global diagnosis and wide-ranging perspectives that his
lecture to the Fabian Society on 'The Irresponsible Society' (delivered
in November 1959) seemed to anticipate. There he declared: 'One of
the most important tasks of socialists in the 1960's will be to re-define
and restate the inherent illogicalities and contradictions in the managerial capitalist system as it is developing within the social structure of
contemporary Britain.'[1] Many will regret that he did not himself
ultimately rise to the challenge; for the fact is that Titmuss promises
more in the way of integration than he in practice provides.

It would, however, be seriously misleading to terminate our evaluation of the work of Richard Titmuss on a negative note. It is no
criticism of an intellectual pioneer to say that he asked more questions
than he answered, and high praise indeed to suggest that he developed
in his novel and original system so useful a framework for examining
social welfare in its social context that it will be modified long before it
is scrapped. Richard Titmuss was a wise and sensitive man who,
because he believed that the truth is the whole, was bound to become
an object of controversy. His critics must, however, be reminded that
they have themselves yet to provide an alternative general theory of
welfare; and that they remain in the vast majority of cases armchair
sailors with boats in the bath in hot pursuit of an energetic self-
educated admiral exploring unknown and uncharted seas in a fleet of
often leaky vessels. One day a system more comprehensive than that

of Titmuss will undoubtedly be developed, for it is in the nature of scientists to benefit from each other's insights and learn from each other's mistakes. Until that day, however, Titmuss' system is vital, for it is the best we have; and even the armchair sailors would not wish for a return to a world of random facts, isolated figures, carefully preserved clippings from the *News* and an anecdote or two about a farmer who behaves like a pig.

Titmuss' system is the best we have. It is also in its own right quite a good system, most notably because it makes two outstanding contributions to the study of the welfare state. These are the following:

1 Social science and social philosophy. Titmuss secured an enviably happy marriage between social science and social philosophy. As a scientist he recognized that the proclamation of principles is no substitute for disciplined thought based on empirical evidence. As a philosopher he returned to the traditional socialist preoccupation with social justice, human equality, citizenship rights, community, compassion and the equitable distribution of power. As a broker between science and philosophy, he believed that men can and do change their minds and then their societies as well; that the driving force behind this change is logic and persuasion; and that bias and ignorance can usually be overcome by informed discussion based on the facts. This missionary zeal to reform society collectively but by peaceful academic means underlies much of his scientific work.

Titmuss stressed that, whether for description or prescription, the facts are essential if meaningful conclusions are to be drawn and useful recommendations made; and he and his colleagues are to be credited with a vast body of scholarly research noteworthy for its high quality and exceptional relevance. For this reason it would be incorrect to say that he and his followers were excessively concerned with policy questions reflecting their own political bias (as some pure academic sociologists have on occasion suggested). It would, however, be true to say that Titmuss did see science as the servant of society; and that many of the questions he asked definitely had moral overtones and were value-laden (questions such as how to eliminate stigma and promote integration, which presuppose that spoiled identity and alienation from the community are always bad by definition rather than demonstration). It would also be true to say that Titmuss sought to reform the public consciousness as a first step towards major social reform. This he succeeded in doing not least through his literary style. His books are provocative and stimulating, even to the general reader;

and the blend of perspectives and principles with a mass of information makes them interesting and often eloquent. They demonstrate how academic methods can shed light on practical problems and prove that ideas do have consequences.

Thus Titmuss' Report in 1961 to the Government of Mauritius, which identified family size and population pressure as that island's main social problem, had far-reaching implications. His recommendations for the three-child family were adopted, and within ten years population growth had fallen dramatically (it was 3.5% p.a. in 1956, for example, but only 1.3% p.a. in 1971).

Again, *Income Distribution and Social Change* proved a valuable and influential attempt to go behind the veil of official statistics and study the social structures which the numbers conceal. In that book Titmuss put his intimate knowledge of the complexities of taxation and insurance to good use and made some significant original calculations and observations. The work may be criticized for the wealth of marginal data that it mobilizes on relatively small abuses (such as the fact that the expense allowance paid to members of the House of Lords is tax-free) and also for its failure to make ambitious original proposals for fiscal reform. It is almost certain, however, that it led directly to the elimination of some of the inequalities perpetuated by the tax system and by the rich who are able to manipulate it; and that it thus played a similar role with respect to relative deprivation to that played at an earlier date by the work of Charles Booth and Seebohm Rowntree with respect to absolute deprivation. Titmuss, Booth and Rowntree, after all, had much in common: all three were not merely collectors of data and sifters of evidence but discontents who used the facts they discovered to attack the complacency of laissez-faire economic and social doctrines, all three explained deprivation (whether absolute or relative) in terms of social causes rather than individual failings, and all three faced the future with an optimism born of belief in the power of persuasion in a humane and democratic society. A reluctance to separate description and prescription, induction and reform is evidently very much part of the British tradition in social policy.

Most spectacularly, *The Gift Relationship* demonstrated statistically the importance of humanitarianism and altruism; showed that compassion is economically efficient where private markets based on self-interest and self-love are not; and actually led to a re-examination of commercial blood-banks in the United States (where the book became a best-seller and prompted Elliott Richardson, then Secretary of State for Health, Education and Welfare, to consult Titmuss personally on questions of reform). The book demonstrated (at least to its author) that values and ideologies display no tendency either to disappear or to converge, and was in many ways the culminating point of Titmuss' lifetime campaign to cajole and convince through rational argument buttressed by hard evidence. It combined useful survey techniques with a comparative approach (albeit mainly with the United States, partly because of the accessibility of information, partly because the strong market orientation of the American Dream served as a tempting target); and it was particularly persuasive by virtue of its multidisciplinary and interdisciplinary perspectives, attempting as it did to break down artificial barriers between economics, sociology, anthropology, philosophy, law and medicine. The resulting synthesis certainly raised both the intellectual level and the moral tone of political argument. Since we have already suggested of that book that, scientifically speaking, the world is in practice probably not as Titmuss there alleged it to be, it is only fair to add that, ethically speaking, it undoubtedly ought to be.

2 The importance of social theory. Titmuss believed that social policy as a subject should do more than simply equip midwives, social workers and other welfare professionals with the skills they would need to treat the symptoms of misery; it should also as a subject learn to explain and predict the incidence and causes of despondency. For this reason he argued that the careful collection of information by itself is no more adequate than *ad hoc* healing; and that a sound body of social theory is the essential precondition for meaningful selection, organization and interpretation of the results of empirical investigation. Titmuss himself attempted to develop such a sound body of theory in the form of a valuable system in which the key concepts are, as we have seen, the following: value consensus, relevance, avoidance of stigma, a universalist infrastructure of welfare services, social costs and social benefits, planned redistribution via selective discrimination, the mixed economy, the failure of the market in welfare matters. This intellectual framework involves structure, function and role, but also ideology and belief, which Titmuss regarded as essential to a young subject where theory had tended to lag behind practice. He warned that 'the social scientist without an ideological frame of reference rarely asks good questions,'[2] and attacked the descriptive and dehumanized approach where 'the "how" and the "why" of social policy, the movement of ideas and forces

which shape social law, are submerged in a mass of factual information. The dilemmas of equity and the conflicts of power are hidden;
what remains is dull and it is comforting.'[3]

Titmuss was a theorist concerned with some of the most fundamental concepts in the sociological tradition, and for this reason never
fully convinces the reader that social policy needs an independent
body of theory of its own. Of course, he was a theorist of intervention
starting from a premise held by hardly any of the Founding Fathers,
that harmonious change presupposes substantial governmental direction; and in arriving at this premise he had been exposed to two
unique recent phenomena, Keynesian economics and the post-war
welfare state. Nonetheless, and apart from the question of state
intervention, it is striking how much of his work was influenced by the
classics, particularly by Durkheim and Weber.

Like Durkheim, Titmuss believed that society is a reality in its own
right (*sui generis*); that social facts can only be explained by reference
to other social facts (and that collective rather than individual causes
and solutions must be found for social problems); and that what
people think is as important as what they do, so that the social
scientist cannot afford to neglect their (subjective) perceptions and
valuations any more than he can afford to neglect their (objective)
behaviour patterns. Like Durkheim, Titmuss recognized that a sense
of resentment could develop where men are not given equal opportunities to fulfil their potential (i.e. where there is a 'forced division of
labour'), but (again like Durkheim) he had little awareness of class
conflict.

Like Durkheim, Titmuss identified the threat of *anomie* (a lack of
sufficient social integration) in a changing industrial society; accepted the existence of social purposes higher than the economic aims of
acquisition and enjoyment; and argued that these social purposes
should be derived from a social value consensus or collective consciousness. Like Durkheim, he noted that economic individualism is
often difficult to reconcile with moral community, while simultaneously recommending that individualism nonetheless be given an
important role to play in the interest of progress. Like Durkheim, he
had little idea of the resources constraint (it is interesting that Titmuss
really only shows awareness of scarcity in work done with Brian Abel-
Smith, a Cambridge economics graduate).

In common with the older Durkheim, Titmuss believed in the
importance of mechanical solidarity (solidarity based on resemblance
rather than on differentiation and interdependence). Both men advo-

cated an institutional remedy to the problem of normlessness; for, just as the school itself (and quite apart from the lessons it provides) has an integrative and socializing function for Durkheim, so the National Health Service and the other institutions of the welfare state have an integrative and socializing function for Titmuss. Both men recommended collective pressures to counteract the threat to the professional ethic from the market mechanism (which by itself is evidently insufficient to ensure standards).

The main difference between Titmuss and Durkheim seems to lie in the nature of provision. Durkheim advocated public education but was prepared to leave many other forms of welfare in the hands of guild-like intermediate groups or 'corporations'. Titmuss, on the other hand, had a wider conception of social welfare, and believed that it should be macrosociological, aimed at the national community and provided by it. Because he believed welfare to be a social rather than a professional or an occupational concern, he would have been adverse to any move towards corporate provision.

As well as with Durkheim, Titmuss shared some of his most fundamental theoretical concepts with Max Weber. Both men believed that science cannot be value-free but that the social scientist should make his personal values clear and attempt to distinguish his empirical evidence from his moral beliefs. Both had a subjectivist and idealist bias, and stressed how often ideas lead to action. Both put bureaucracy at the centre of their model (Germany in the time of Weber already had a welfare state, and it was itself highly bureaucratized); and both emphasized that private sector bureaucracies are no less bureaucratic than state sector bureaucracies. Both believed in the need for a nation to identify collective ends, and both hence tended to assign an important role to the political leadership.

Both Titmuss and Weber liked history for its own sake and as a guide to the future. Both were scrupulous collectors and collators of information, but neither was afraid to draw lessons from the data or mobilize facts in the service of a political cause. Both were generalists who attempted to integrate economy and society into a multidisciplinary matrix.

If he was influenced positively by Durkheim and Weber, Titmuss was influenced negatively by liberal utilitarianism and exchange theory. He found ideas of individual (consumer) sovereignty, laissez-faire, natural self-interest repellent; refused to use the isolated individual (say, 'economic man') as his unit of analysis; and was thus hostile to the market mechanism on ethical and sociological as well as, of course, strictly economic grounds. It is important to realize that he regarded the liberal utilitarian positivist theory of action of the economics textbook not merely as different in normative orientation from the unilaterality of transfers in the welfare sector, but as inferior to it.

If Titmuss was influenced negatively by liberal utilitarianism, then it would be true to say that he was hardly influenced at all by Marx. Marxian ideas such as the basis/superstructure relationship, exploitation, class conflict or the limitations of parliamentary socialism are conspicuous by their absence. So too is serious discussion of alienation at the place of work, or any hint that denial of participation in decision-making or of the opportunity to feel creative could be the cause of many of the problems treated in the welfare sector.

Titmuss was not a Marxist because of his strong faith in parliamentary democracy; and because the metaphysical speculation and massive system-building of the Marxists would have appealed to him as little as did Parsonian 'grand theory'. Through his distaste for Marxism, Titmuss helped to preserve the traditional link in Britain between social welfare and democratic socialism.

It is too easily forgotten that British socialism, unlike some of its continental counterparts, has its roots not in *Das Kapital* but in the Tolpuddle martyrs and the chapels of South Wales. Like many other British socialists, Titmuss was writing in the shadow of the Bible, with its emphasis on community, responsibility, duty, sin, guilt and its stress that the act of giving is somehow good in itself. Perhaps in the last analysis Titmuss can only fully be understood if one interprets his life's work as an attempt to find a collective response to Cain's perceptive question on the nature of social welfare: 'Am I my brother's keeper?'

Ethically opposed to uhc
Writing as a Christian socialist.

Reference Notes

CHAPTER ONE

1 *CW*, p. 7.
2 R. M. Titmuss, *Poverty and Population* (London: Macmillan and Co., 1938), pp. x–xi.
3 M. Gowing, 'Richard Morris Titmuss', *Proceedings of the British Academy*, Vol. LXI (1975), p. 29.
4 R. H. Tawney, 'The War and the People', *New Statesman and Nation*, 22nd April 1950, p. 454. It is indicative of Titmuss' anonymity in 1950 that Tawney throughout the seven-column review article consistently misspells his name.
5 Gowing, op. cit., p. 27.

CHAPTER TWO

1 *SP*, p. 24.
2 *SP*, p. 131.
3 *SP*, p. 27.
4 *SP*, p. 16.
5 *SP*, p. 22.
6 *SP*, p. 16.
7 *EWS*, p. 39.
8 *CW*, p. 22.
9 *CW*, p. 131.
10 *SP*, pp. 57–8.
11 *EWS*, p. 42.
12 *EWS*, p. 42.
13 *SP*, p. 141.
14 *EWS*, p. 39.
15 *EWS*, p. 40.
16 *CW*, p. 81.

17 *EWS*, p. 40.
18 *CW*, p. 93.
19 R. M. Titmuss, 'Goals of Today's Welfare State', in P. Anderson and R. Blackburn (eds.), *Towards Socialism* (London: Fontana, 1965, p. 354).
20 *EWS*, pp. 22–3.
21 *PSP*, p. 133.
22 *EWS*, p. 85.
23 *PSP*, p. 506.
24 *PSP*, p. 507.
25 *PSP*, pp. 506–7.
26 *PSP*, p. 508.
27 *PSP*, p. 511.
28 *PSP*, p. 508.
29 R. M. Titmuss, Introduction to R. H. Tawney, *Equality* (London: George Allen and Unwin Ltd., 1964), p. 10.
30 *GR*, pp. 196–7.
31 *GR*, p. 196.
32 *GR*, p. 196.
33 Introduction to *Equality*, p. 14.
34 Introduction to *Equality*, p. 14.
35 *SP*, p. 16.
36 *SP*, p. 136.
37 *CW*, p. 69.
38 *SP*, p. 52.
39 *CW*, p. 185.
40 *SPPGM*, p. 187.
41 *HST*, p. 95.
42 *SPPGM*, p. 107.
43 *SPPGM*, pp. 130–1.
44 *SPPGM*, p. 135.
45 *SPPGM*, pp. 136–7.
46 *SPPGM*, p. 130.
47 *SPPGM*, p. 242.
48 *SPPGM*, p. 182.
49 *SPPGM*, p. 182.
50 *GR*, p. 180.
51 *GR*, p. 224.
52 *GR*, p. 224.
53 *GR*, p. 224.
54 *GR*, p. 225.
55 *GR*, p. 224.
56 *EWS*, p. 20.
57 *CW*, p. 35.
58 *GR*, p. 253.
59 *CW*, p. 151.
60 *GR*, p. 212.
61 *SP*, p. 27.
62 *CW*, p. 116.
63 *SP*, p. 103.

64 Introduction to *Equality*, p. 14.

CHAPTER THREE

1 *SP*, p. 15.
2 *SP*, p. 57.
3 *SP*, p. 51.
4 *CW*, p. 21.
5 *SP*, p. 51.
6 *CW*, p. 13.
7 *CW*, p. 18.
8 *EWS*, p. 111.
9 *CW*, p. 41.
10 *CW*, p. 72.
11 *CW*, p. 85.
12 *CW*, p. 41.
13 *PSP*, p. 218.
14 *PSP*, p. 342.
15 *CW*, p. 29.
16 *CW*, p. 34.
17 *CW*, p. 31.
18 *CW*, p. 29.
19 *CW*, p. 52.
20 *CW*, p. 20.
21 *CW*, p. 19.
22 *IS*, p. 221.
23 *IS*, p. 222.
24 *SP*, p. 66.
25 'Goals of Today's Welfare State', p. 355.
26 *CW*, p. 25.
27 *CW*, p. 14.
28 *CW*, p. 39.
29 *CW*, p. 42.
30 'Goals of Today's Welfare State', p. 354.
31 'Goals of Today's Welfare State', p. 362.
32 *CW*, p. 43.
33 *PSP*, p. 88.
34 *CW*, p. 104.
35 *SP*, p. 52.
36 *SP*, p. 53.
37 *SP*, pp. 53–4.
38 *CW*, p. 31.
39 *GR*, p. 223.
40 *GR*, p. 223.
41 *CW*, p. 40.
42 *EWS*, p. 33.

CHAPTER FOUR

1 *CW*, p. 18.

2 *CW*, p. 22.
3 *CW*, p. 150.
4 R. M. Titmuss, 'Social Security and the Six', *New Society*, 11th November 1971, p. 929.
5 *EWS*, pp. 8–9.
6 *GR*, p. 272.
7 *PSP*, p. 46.
8 T. H. Marshall, 'Value Problems of Welfare-Capitalism', *Journal of Social Policy*, January 1972, p. 24.
9 *CW*, p. 195.
10 G. Myrdal, *Beyond the Welfare State* (London: Methuen, 1960), pp. 63–4.
11 M. Friedman, *Capitalism and Freedom* (Chicago: The University of Chicago Press, 1962), p. 15.
12 *PSP*, p. 105.
13 *EWS*, p. 29.
14 *EWS*, p. 33.
15 *SPPGM*, p. 93.

CHAPTER FIVE

1 *CW*, pp. 20, 64; *SP*, p. 58.
2 E. Goffman, *Stigma: Notes on the Management of Spoiled Identity* (Harmondsworth: Penguin Books, 1970).
3 *SP*, p. 44.
4 *CW*, p. 26.
5 *CW*, p. 86.
6 *CW*, pp. 89, 98–9.
7 *IS*, p. 236.
8 Introduction to *Equality*, p. 16.
9 *CW*, p. 155.
10 *CW*, p. 134.
11 *CW*, p. 134.
12 *CW*, p. 163.
13 *CW*, p. 129.
14 *CW*, p. 119.
15 *CW*, p. 163.
16 *CW*, p. 132.
17 *CW*, p. 119.
18 *CW*, p. 121.
19 *CW*, p. 120.
20 *CW*, p. 120.
21 *CW*, p. 134.
22 *CW*, p. 143.
23 *CW*, p. 143.
24 *CW*, p. 113.
25 *SP*, p. 46.

CHAPTER SIX

1 *EWS*, p. 19.

2 *SP*, pp. 45–6.
3 R. Pinker, *Social Theory and Social Policy* (London: Heinemann Educational Books, 1971), pp. 141–2.
4 R. M. Titmuss, 'Superannuation For All: A Broader View'. *New Society*, 27th February 1969, p. 315.

CHAPTER SEVEN

1 *SP*, p. 67.
2 *CW*, p. 63.
3 *CW*, p. 156.
4 *EWS*, p. 112.
5 *EWS*, p. 112.
6 *EWS*, p. 108.
7 *EWS*, p. 109.
8 *PSP*, pp. 216–17.
9 *PSP*, p. 335.
10 *CW*, p. 157.
11 *CW*, p. 133.
12 *CW*, p. 133.
13 *SP*, p. 89.
14 *CW*, p. 133.
15 *PSP*, p. 382.
16 *SP*, p. 133.
17 *SP*, p. 133.
18 *CW*, p. 163.
19 *CW*, p. 164.
20 *CW*, p. 157.
21 *CW*, p. 158.
22 *CW*, p. 63.
23 *CW*, p. 134.
24 *CW*, p. 133.
25 *SP*, pp. 75–6.
26 *SP*, p. 84.
27 *GR*, p. 43.
28 *SP*, p. 83.
29 'Goals of Today's Welfare State', p. 355.
30 *EWS*, pp. 8–9.
31 *SPPGM*, p. 228.
32 *SP*, p. 65.
33 *SP*, p. 65.
34 *SP*, pp. 65–6.
35 *SP*, p. 67.

CHAPTER EIGHT

1 *SP*, p. 38.
2 *CW*, p. 131.
3 *CW*, p. 22.
4 *HST*, p. 171.

5 *PSP*, p. 347.
6 *SP*, p. 141.
7 *HST*, p. 214.
8 *CW*, p. 182.
9 *SP*, p. 38.
10 *CW*, p. 191.
11 *IS*, p. 218.
12 *SP*, p. 38.
13 *CW*, p. 142.
14 *CW*, p. 195.
15 *CW*, p. 196.
16 *EWS*, p. 37.
17 *SP*, p. 14.
18 *CW*, p. 66.
19 *CW*, p. 45.
20 *EWS*, p. 74.
21 *CW*, p. 71.
22 R. M. Titmuss, 'Welfare "Rights", Law and Discretion', *The Political Quarterly*, April–May 1971, p. 116.
23 'Welfare "Rights", Law and Discretion', p. 126.
24 'Welfare "Rights", Law and Discretion', pp. 124–5.
25 'Welfare "Rights", Law and Discretion', p. 127.
26 'Welfare "Rights", Law and Discretion', p. 116.
27 *CW*, p. 22.
28 *GR*, p. 17.
29 *GR*, p. 16.
30 *GR*, p. 276.
31 *GR*, p. 201.
32 *GR*, p. 223.
33 *GR*, p. 147.
34 *GR*, p. 146.
35 *GR*, pp. 149–50.
36 *GR*, p. 266.
37 *GR*, p. 268.
38 *GR*, pp. 254–5.
39 *GR*, p. 268.
40 *GR*, p. 223.
41 *GR*, p. 17.
42 *GR*, p. 16.
43 *GR*, p. 171.
44 See M. Mauss, *The Gift* (London: Cohen and West, 1954), and C. Lévi-Strauss, *The Elementary Structures of Kinship* (London: Eyre and Spottiswoode, 1969).
45 *GR*, p. 82.
46 *GR*, p. 269.
47 *GR*, p. 269.
48 *GR*, p. 239.
49 *GR*, p. 241.
50 *GR*, p. 242.

51 *GR*, p. 242.
52 *GR*, p. 243.
53 *GR*, p. 180.

CHAPTER NINE

 1 *CW*, p. 189.
 2 *CW*, p. 65.
 3 'Goals of Today's Welfare State', p. 360.
 4 *CW*, p. 162.
 5 *CW*, pp. 193–4.
 6 *IDSC*, p. 79. These figures refer to 1959.
 7 *IDSC*, p. 89.
 8 *IDSC*, p. 188.
 9 *IDSC*, p. 198.
10 'Goals of Today's Welfare State', p. 360.
11 *CW*, pp. 32–3.
12 *CW*, p. 32.
13 'Goals of Today's Welfare State', p. 359.
14 Introduction to *Equality*, p. 12.
15 'Goals of Today's Welfare State', p. 360.
16 'Goals of Today's Welfare State', p. 363.
17 *CW*, p. 196.
18 *EWS*, pp. 208–9.
19 *GR*, p. 153.
20 *CW*, p. 67.
21 *IS*, p. 230.
22 *EWS*, p. 51.
23 *IS*, p. 230.
24 *EWS*, p. 73.
25 *SPPGM*, p. 6.
26 *CW*, p. 192.
27 *EWS*, p. 55.
28 *CW*, p. 197.
29 *CW*, p. 135.
30 Introduction to *Equality*, p. 9.
31 *CW*, p. 164.
32 Introduction to *Equality*, pp. 9–10.
33 *PSP*, p. 348.
34 *PSP*, p. 346.
35 *CW*, p. 114.
36 'Goals of Today's Welfare State', p. 365.
37 *CW*, p. 92.
38 *CW*, p. 182.
39 *CW*, p. 135.
40 *CW*, p. 135.
41 *CW*, p. 159.
42 *CW*, p. 121.
43 *IDSC*, p. 197

44 *CW*, p. 114.
45 *CW*, p. 184.
46 *CW*, p. 122.
47 *CW*, p. 184.
48 *CW*, pp. 121–2.
49 *CW*, p. 114.
50 *CW*, p. 135.
51 *CW*, p. 114.
52 *CW*, p. 33.
53 *CW*, p. 34.
54 *CW*, p. 34.
55 *CW*, p. 34.
56 *CW*, p. 34.
57 Introduction to *Equality*, pp. 22–3.
58 Introduction to *Equality*, p. 24.
59 *SP*, p. 104.
60 *SP*, p. 106.
61 *SP*, p. 103.
62 *SPPGM*, p. 110.
63 'Superannuation for All: A Broader View', p. 316.
64 'Superannuation for All: A Broader View', p. 316.
65 *EWS*, p. 94.
66 *SPPGM*, p. 100.
67 *SPPGM*, p. 140.
68 'Goals of Today's Welfare State', p. 362.
69 Introduction to *Equality*, pp. 11–12.
70 *EWS*, p. 105.
71 *SP*, p. 25.
72 *SP*, p. 25.
73 *EWS*, p. 20.
74 *SP*, pp. 24–5.

CHAPTER TEN
 1 *SP*, p. 31.
 2 *SPPGM*, p. 105.
 3 *SP*, p. 89.
 4 *CW*, pp. 63, 118, 131.
 5 R. M. Titmuss, 'The Welfare State: Images and Realities', in C. I. Schott-land, ed., *The Welfare State* (New York: Harper Torchbooks, 1967), p. 100.
 6 'The Welfare State: Images and Realities', p. 100.
 7 Introduction to *Equality*, p. 13.
 8 *SP*, p. 133.
 9 *EWS*, p. 109.
10 *EWS*, p. 109.
11 *EWS*, p. 116.
12 *EWS*, pp. 117–18.
13 G. Myrdal, 'The Place of Values in Social Policy', *Journal of Social Policy*, January 1972, pp. 6–7.

14 *EWS*, p. 181.
15 *EWS*, p. 182.
16 *EWS*, p. 198.
17 *EWS*, p. 198.
18 *CW*, p. 191.
19 *GR*, p. 223.
20 *GR*, p. 102.
21 *SPPGM*, pp. 93–4.
22 *HST*, p. 214.
23 P. Marris and P. Rein. *Dilemmas of Social Reform* (Harmondsworth: Penguin Books, 1974), p. 101.
24 'Goals of Today's Welfare State', p. 359.
25 *EWS*, p. 74.
26 R. M. Titmuss, 'A Commentary', in W. J. Braithwaite, *Lloyd George's Ambulance Wagon* (London: Methuen and Co. Ltd., 1957), p. 56.
27 *EWS*, p. 39.

CHAPTER ELEVEN

1 *GR*, p. 109.
2 *CW*, pp. 134–5.
3 *GR*, p. 166.
4 *GR*, p. 164.
5 *GR*, p. 163.
6 *GR*, pp. 270–1.
7 *GR*, p. 271.
8 *CW*, p. 151.
9 GR, p. 109.
10 *GR*, p. 169.
11 *GR*, pp. 27, 175.
12 *GR*, p. 175.
13 *GR*, p. 277.
14 *GR*, p. 178.
15 *CW*, pp. 224–5.
16 *SPPGM*, p. 35; *CW*, pp. 226, 253.
17 *CW*, p. 257.
18 *CW*, p. 257.
19 *SPPGM*, p. 177.
20 *CW*, p. 250.
21 *CW*, p. 254.
22 *CW*, p. 255.
23 *CW*, p. 254.
24 *CW*, p. 222.
25 *GR*, p. 188.
26 *GR*, p. 189.
27 *CW*, p. 254.
28 *CW*, p. 254.
29 *GR*, p. 188.
30 *CW*, p. 260.

31 *CW*, p. 208.
32 *SP*, p. 56.
33 *SP*, p. 56.
34 *SPPGM*, p. 196.
35 *HST*, p. 212. See also *EWS*, pp. 159, 161, 189.
36 *GR*, p. 193.
37 *GR*, p. 193.
38 *HST*, p. 69.
39 *HST*, p. 101.
40 *EWS*, p. 200.
41 *HST*, p. 69.
42 *CW*, p. 225.
43 *CW*, p. 255.
44 *CW*, p. 208.
45 *CW*, p. 255.
46 *EWS*, pp. 124–5.
47 *EWS*, p. 126.
48 *CW*, p. 210.
49 *CW*, p. 73.
50 *CW*, pp. 73–4.
51 *CW*, p. 250.
52 *CW*, p. 71.
53 *CW*, p. 70.
54 *CW*, p. 213.
55 *CW*, p. 208.
56 *EWS*, p. 193.
57 *EWS*, p. 191.

CHAPTER TWELVE

 1 *CW*, p. 91.
 2 *SP*, p. 55.
 3 *CW*, pp. 67–8.
 4 *CW*, p. 184.
 5 *IS*, p. 238.
 6 *IS*, p. 240.
 7 *IS*, p. 236.
 8 *SP*, p. 112.
 9 *CW*, p. 178.
10 *CW*, p. 179.
11 *CW*, p. 183.
12 *CW*, p. 180.
13 *CW*, p. 179.
14 *SP*, p. 92.
15 *SP*, p. 98.
16 *CW*, p. 193.
17 *CW*, p. 181.
18 *IS*, p. 241.
19 'A Commentary', in W. J. Braithwaite, *Lloyd George's Ambulance Wagon*, p. 53.

20 *EWS*, p. 28.
21 *IS*, p. 216.
22 *EWS*, p. 121.
23 *CW*, p. 196.
24 *EWS*, p. 155.
25 *EWS*, p. 197.
26 *EWS*, p. 196.
27 *EWS*, p. 197.
28 *CW*, p. 212.
29 *CW*, p. 184.
30 *HST*, pp. 202–3.
31 *EWS*, pp. 119, 120.
32 *SP*, p. 14.
33 *SP*, p. 42, See also pp. 34, 130.
34 *CW*, p. 196.
35 *EWS*, p. 27.
36 *EWS*, p. 27.
37 'Goals of Today's Welfare State', p. 364.
38 *EWS*, p. 190.
39 *EWS*, p. 128.
40 *EWS*, p. 183.
41 *EWS*, p. 130.
42 *HST*, p. 145.
43 *HST*, p. 146.
44 *HST*, p. 146.
45 *HST*, p. 101.

CHAPTER THIRTEEN

1 *CW*, p. 252.
2 *CW*, p. 253.
3 *CW*, p. 254.
4 *GR*, p. 249.
5 *CW*, p. 254.
6 *CW*, p. 254.
7 *CW*, p. 268.
8 *PSP*, pp. 70–1.
9 *PSP*, p. 71.
10 *CW*, p. 254.
11 *HST*, p. 102.
12 *HST*, p. 111.
13 *HST*, p. 110.
14 *HST*, p. 100.
15 *HST*, p. 215.
16 *CW*, p. 149.
17 *GR*, p. 221.
18 *CW*, p. 150.
19 *GR*, p. 38.
20 *GR*, p. 49.

21 *GR*, p. 234.
22 *IS*, p. 229.
23 Introduction to *Equality*, p. 9.
24 *CW*, p. 76.

CHAPTER FOURTEEN

1 *CW*, p. 252.
2 *CW*, p. 254.
3 *CW*, p. 253.
4 *CW*, p. 151.
5 *CW*, p. 258.
6 *SP*, p. 82.
7 *CW*, p. 122.
8 *GR*, p. 232.
9 *GR*, p. 221.
10 *GR*, p. 57.
11 *GR*, p. 66.
12 *GR*, p. 73.
13 *CW*, p. 252.
14 *CW*, p. 255.

CHAPTER FIFTEEN

1 *HST*, p. 99.
2 *HST*, p. 165.
3 *HST*, p. 166.
4 *HST*, p. 159.
5 *Cost*, p. 59.
6 *CW*, p. 138.
7 *CW*, p. 20.
8 *EWS*, p. 126.
9 *CW*, p. 266.
10 *SP*, p. 82.
11 Introduction to *Equality*, p. 10.
12 Tawney, *Equality*, p. 81.
13 Ibid., p. 40.
14 R. M. Titmuss, 'Social Welfare and the Art of Giving', in E. Fromm, ed., *Socialist Humanism* (London: Allen Lane, 1967), pp. 358–9.
15 *SP*, p. 29.

CHAPTER SIXTEEN

1 *IS*, p. 215.
2 R. M. Titmuss, Foreword to M. Rein, *Social Policy* (New York: Random House, 1970), p. v.
3 R. M. Titmuss, 'Historical Sedatives', *New Statesman*, 16 June 1961, p. 962.

Index